CAREER OPPORTUNITIES IN HEALTH CARE MANAGEMENT

Perspectives from the Field

Sharon B. Buchbinder, RN, PhD
Professor and Chair
Department of Health Science
Towson University
Towson, Maryland

Jon M. Thompson, PhD
Professor and Director
Health Services Administration Program
James Madison University
Harrisonburg, Virginia

JONES AND BARTLETT PUBLISHERS
Sudbury, Massachusetts
BOSTON   TORONTO   LONDON   SINGAPORE

World Headquarters

Jones and Bartlett Publishers	Jones and Bartlett Publishers	Jones and Bartlett Publishers
40 Tall Pine Drive	Canada	International
Sudbury, MA 01776	6339 Ormindale Way	Barb House, Barb Mews
978-443-5000	Mississauga, Ontario L5V 1J2	London W6 7PA
info@jbpub.com	Canada	United Kingdom
www.jbpub.com		

Jones and Bartlett's books and products are available through most bookstores and online book-sellers. To contact Jones and Bartlett Publishers directly, call 800-832-0034, fax 978-443-8000, or visit our website, www.jbpub.com.

Substantial discounts on bulk quantities of Jones and Bartlett's publications are available to corporations, professional associations, and other qualified organizations. For details and specific discount information, contact the special sales department at Jones and Bartlett via the above contact information or send an email to specialsales@jbpub.com.

This publication is designed to provide accurate and authoritative information in regard to the Subject Matter covered. It is sold with the understanding that the publisher is not engaged in rendering legal, accounting, or other professional service. If legal advice or other expert assistance is required, the service of a competent professional person should be sought.

Production Credits

Publisher: Michael Brown
Production Director: Amy Rose
Editorial Assistant: Catie Heverling
Editorial Assistant: Teresa Reilly
Senior Production Editor: Tracey Chapman
Associate Production Editor: Kate Stein
Senior Marketing Manager: Sophie Fleck
Manufacturing and Inventory Control
  Supervisor: Amy Bacus

Composition: Publishers' Design & Production
  Services, Inc.
Art: Publishers' Design & Production Services, Inc.
Cover Design: Kristin E. Parker
Cover Image: © Alain Lacroix/Dreamstime.com
Printing and Binding: Malloy, Inc.
Cover Printing: Malloy, Inc.

Library of Congress Cataloging-in-Publication Data
Buchbinder, Sharon Bell.
   Career opportunities in health care management : perspectives from the field / Sharon B. Buchbinder and Jon M. Thompson.
      p. cm.
   ISBN-13: 978-0-7637-5964-3 (pbk.)
   ISBN-10: 0-7637-5964-3 (pbk.)
   1. Health services administrators—Vocational guidance. I. Thompson, Jon M. II. Title.
   RA971.B893 2010
   362.1023—dc22

                                                                                    2009003675

6048

Printed in the United States of America
13 12 11 10 09   10 9 8 7 6 5 4 3 2 1

Dedication

We dedicate this book to our loving spouses, Dale Buchbinder
and Suzanne Gilchrist-Thompson,
who kept asking:
"ARE YOU DONE YET?"

Contents

Preface ix

Foreword by Quint Studer xi

Foreword by Leonard H. Friedman xiii

About the Authors xv

Acknowledgments xvii

Chapter 1 The Healthcare Management Workforce 1

Why Choose Healthcare Management? 2

The Origins of Healthcare Management 3

Growth and Opportunities .3

Healthcare Management Talent Quotient Quiz 5

Knowledge Base Required for Healthcare
    Management 7

Managerial Skills Required for Healthcare
    Management 9

Experiential Learning Required for Healthcare
    Management 12

Chapter Summary 13

Chapter 2 Understanding Healthcare Management 17

The Need for Management and Their Perspective . . .18

Management: Definition, Functions, and
    Competencies 19

Management Positions: The Control in the
    Organizational Hierarchy 21

Focus of Management: Self, Unit/Team, and
    Organization 24

Role of the Manager in Talent Management 26

Role of the Manager in Ensuring High
Performance 26
Role of the Manager in Succession Planning 28
Chapter Summary 29

Chapter 3 **Healthcare Management Practice Settings 33**
Understanding Practice Settings: Direct and
Non-Direct Care 33
Direct Care Settings 34
Ambulatory Care Organizations/Clinics 34
Health Departments: Local, County, State,
and Federal 36
Hospitals 40
Hospital Systems 42
Physician Practices 44
Assisted Living Facilities 48
Nursing Homes 50
Retirement Communities 53
Wellness/Fitness Centers 55
Non-Direct Care Settings 57
Associations 57
Consulting Firms 59
Medical Suppliers 61
Managed Care Organizations/Health Insurers 63
Pharmaceutical Firms 65

Chapter 4 **Perspectives from the Field: Profiles
of Healthcare Managers .71**
Sampling Matrix and Process for Developing
Profiles 72
A Day in the Life of Healthcare Managers 73
Proportion of Time Spent on Management Functions 73
Use of Knowledge, Skills, and Abilities 74
Key Sources of Satisfaction 75
Profiles of Healthcare Managers 77
Larry M. Beck, MBA, MHA, FACHE 78
Michael C. Boblitz, MBA 81
Sandy Cave, RN, BSN 84
Stephanie Chisolm, PhD 87
Kristi Donovan, MS, CAE 90
Teresa L. Edwards, MHA, FACHE 93
Christopher Fanning, MHSA .96

Valerie Fearns 98
William J. Forbes, PhD 102
Harry Fox 104
Treg Fuller, MSS 106
Schuyler Fury 108
Theresa C. Honchar, LPN 112
Andrew Jones, MS 114
J. S. Parker Jones, IV, MS, CNHA, FACHCA 117
Michael Jurgensen, MHA 120
Sharon E. Kelley, RN, MS, NEA-BC 122
Mary Beth Kiser, MPH 125
Lauren Koontz 127
Jim Krauss, MHSA, FACHE 129
Amanda Llewellyn, MHA/MBA, FACHE 131
Jerod M. Loeb, PhD 135
Lew Lyon, PhD 137
Natassja Manzanero 140
Karen Maust 144
Michael J. McDonnell, MBA .147
Matt Neiswanger, MSW, LNHA 150
Ryan Novak 153
Ryan Papa 156
Reena Patel 160
Justine Powell 162
Jeff Richardson, MBA, LCSW-C 165
Andrea Saevoon 167
Jennifer R. Shapiro, MPH 169
Sunil K. Sinha, MD, MBA, FACHE 171
Justin E. Skinner, MFA, MBA 174
Wes Street, NHA 176
Richard J. Stull, FACHE 178
Jeanine Tyler 181
Jennifer Villani, MPH 184
Jason Vollmer 187
Tanisha Woodard 191

Chapter 5   **Summary and Conclusions About
the Profession** **195**
Themes from the Healthcare Manager Profiles 195
Interest in the Profession and Satisfaction 196
The Role of Mentors 197
Variation in Preparation, Experiences, and Roles 198
Challenges Faced by Healthcare Managers 199

Growth Areas for Healthcare Management 200
Skills Needed for the Next Generation of
    Healthcare Managers 202
Advice from the Managers .204
Conclusions 206

Appendix A   **Resources for Learning More About Healthcare
Management 207**
Acronyms, Organizations, and Web Addresses 207

Appendix B   **Sample Bachelor of Science Healthcare Management
Programs of Study 211**
James Madison University .211
Towson University 215

Appendix C   **Sample Master of Health Administration (MHA)
Degree Requirements 219**
The Pennsylvania State University 219

Appendix D   **Getting a Job in Healthcare Management 221**
Frequently Asked Questions (FAQs) 221
Commonly Used Terms in Job Advertising and Position
    Descriptions 224
Sample Position Descriptions 227
Do's and Don'ts of Interviewing 229
Checklist for Finding the Right Job 233
Sample Cover Letters and Résumés 235

Index 243

Preface

Every good book begins with a vision. Having taught and mentored healthcare management students for almost two decades, we recognize that students yearn for guidance in making the specific connection between the *profession* of healthcare management and *career opportunities* they could consider. Since no current book like this exists, we decided to write one. That was our vision—to develop a helpful, reader-friendly book based on the real-world stories of practicing managers that would inform students about the opportunities within healthcare management, as well as inspire those interested in becoming future healthcare managers.

To carry out our vision, we chose to describe specific areas and levels of employment in the book so readers would have a sense of what healthcare managers do in a given setting at a particular point in their career. To ensure proper coverage of the field, we created a matrix and identified the settings we wanted to represent in our sample and strove to find a person for each setting at the supervisor/line or staff, mid-level/director, or executive/senior level of his or her career. Then we used an online program to launch the survey.

We are extremely pleased with the results. We invited 52 healthcare managers to participate; 42 completed the survey, reviewed their profiles, and granted written permission to publish them. This excellent response rate of 81% was due, in large part, to the power of our relationships with the participants: alumni of our programs, colleagues in professional organizations, preceptors for our student interns, and past coworkers who gave generously of their time, expertise, and wisdom. They did this out of a deep commitment to the field of healthcare management and as a gift to future students. We are deeply grateful to our participants for their great generosity of time and expertise. This book would not have been possible without them.

Career Opportunities in Health Care Management: Perspectives from the Field is a concise, reader-friendly, introductory healthcare management book that covers a wide variety of career opportunities in a broad range of direct healthcare settings, such as hospitals, physician practices, nursing homes, and clinics, and non-direct healthcare settings, such as associations, health insurance companies, medical suppliers, and consulting firms. Filled with first-person accounts from healthcare managers working in the field, these profiles will engage the reader's imagination, inform them of key issues associated with these important roles, as well as what makes these healthcare managers happy and eager to go to work in the morning. Beginning with an individualized Healthcare Management Talent Quotient Quiz and ending with a guide to finding a job in healthcare management, this hands-on, student-friendly and teacher-friendly text is the perfect resource for students of healthcare management, nursing, allied health, business administration, pharmacy, occupational therapy, public administration, and public health. Along with dynamic writing and stories from real healthcare managers, this book features:

- Chapters written by experienced authors using an active voice to grab the reader's attention.
- An individualized Healthcare Management Talent Quotient Quiz to assess each student's baseline aptitude and identify skills gaps that need to be addressed.
- Over 40 lively, first-person profiles of healthcare managers working in the field covering everything from educational background and how they first became interested in healthcare management, to advice for future healthcare managers.
- Detailed appendices that include resources for learning more about healthcare management; sample programs of study; job-hunting advice; frequently used terms in job advertisements; sample position descriptions; do's and don'ts of interviewing; and sample cover letters and résumés.

We hope you enjoy reading this book as much as we enjoyed bringing it together. At every step along the way, we asked ourselves, "What did I need in the classroom when I started teaching—and didn't have?" May you and your students be excited by the plethora of opportunities waiting for them in the dynamic field of healthcare management, and may your graduates bring back stories for future generations.

Sharon B. Buchbinder, RN, PhD   Jon M. Thompson, PhD
Towson University   James Madison University

Foreword

Quint Studer

Thank you for writing a "how-to" book. The healthcare field tends to attract many books that have value in reference to why something needs to be done. There are countless books on what needs to be done. Even books on who should do it. So with all these books covering the why, what, and by whom, why is it we do not have consistent excellence in health care? Yes, we have those pockets of excellence, such as the great Heart Institute or an organization at the top of its specialty for a period of time, but few organizations gain and sustain that excellence.

So what is the vital factor in making health care's future bright? Lives depend on it. The field is attracting, developing, and recruiting talent. This, combined with the right position, will create great health care. This book facilitates the above and more.

I like the way the book is organized. Chapter 1 is the diagnosis. Using healthcare terms, how can we make the right selection and create the right treatment plan without the right diagnosis? I love the Healthcare Management Talent Quotient Quiz. After completing a diagnostic workup, the next step is to investigate the best treatment to maximize the patient's outcome. The goal and far reaches of this book are to maximize our human potential. Chapter 2 guides the reader through this investigation. Chapter 3 allows the reader to dig deeper into this research and develop his or her own educated treatment plan to see what setting will fit his or her passion and potential. Chapter 4 brings the reader to closure in this investigation with the profiles of people who are already in the field.

Health care is blessed in that people with great passion are attracted to this field. *Career Opportunities in Health Care Management: Perspectives from the Field* helps guide this passion so that the reason why someone enters this career is not lost: making a positive difference in the lives of others.

Thank you, Dr. Buchbinder and Dr. Thompson, for writing this book, which will make health care better.

Quint Studer
Founder and CEO
The Studer Group
Gulf Breeze, Florida

Foreword

Leonard H. Friedman

I would like to begin this foreword with a brief story that speaks clearly as to why healthcare management as a career is so important and absolutely vital to the health of both individuals and communities. Several years ago, one of my colleagues suffered a heart attack. His heart attack was so severe that when he was admitted to the emergency department of the local hospital in our community and an angiogram was performed, it was determined that all five main coronary arteries needed to be replaced right then. Fortunately, the local hospital had recently built a heart center and staffed it with two experienced cardiac surgeons along with the other staff and equipment needed to perform coronary artery bypass graft surgeries. The quintuple bypass was performed that evening and my colleague survived.

Some months later, I saw him at one of the local coffee shops and I asked him how he was doing, at which time he shared something with me that I have never forgotten. He told me how in the days and weeks after his surgery, he discovered why healthcare management is so important. When I asked him to elaborate, he mentioned that had the CEO and board of the local health system not made the decision to build the heart center, he would have certainly died given that the next closest hospital with the staff and facilities to do heart surgery was 45 miles away. The vision and wisdom of that system CEO saved the life of my colleague.

There is absolutely no question that healthcare organizations need highly skilled and dedicated clinicians to deliver the kind of safe and effective care that each and every person needs and deserves. Whether that person is a physician, nurse, therapist, technologist, or other direct or indirect caregiver, health care is absolutely dependent on these amazing people. However, equally amazing is the role that healthcare management plays in creating and sustaining the systems that allow clinicians and caregivers to do their very best work. Without healthcare managers at all levels of their organizations, the actual delivery of care would be severely compromised. Think about the breadth of what healthcare managers do including:

- Craft a vision for what their organization can become
- Identify healthcare needs in the community and bring the right resources to address those needs
- Manage complex businesses that are often the largest part of the economy in many communities
- Lead at all levels of their organizations
- Manage relationships with multiple stakeholder groups

Healthcare management is not a career for persons who want a smooth and steady job that stays the same from one day to the next. Persons in this field not only have to be comfortable with change, they have to be change agents—creating an intentional future and continually motivating others toward that future. Healthcare managers have to be stewards of the financial, technical, and human resources for which they are responsible. Above all else, healthcare management is a people business. The best healthcare managers are those who understand that relationships truly matter. They think clearly and listen carefully. They are action-oriented people who also take the time to think through the consequences of their options. They know in their core that healthcare management is about service to others—people who use their services (let us call them "patients" for a moment) and are very frequently sick, vulnerable, and frightened. Healthcare managers have an opportunity to make a difference in the lives of patients, their families, and their communities.

My hope is that as you go through this superb book, you will think about what healthcare management does. Read the stories of those who have dedicated their lives to this career and you will understand why healthcare managers make such a profound difference in their organizations and the communities they serve. As you go through the book think about my colleague who would not be alive today were it not for a wise and forward-thinking healthcare executive. This is truly a career in which you can make a significant difference and touch the lives of persons in ways you might not have thought possible.

Leonard H. Friedman, PhD, MPH
Professor and Director
The George Washington University
Department of Health Services Management and Leadership

About the Authors

Sharon B. Buchbinder, RN, PhD

Professor and Chair
Department of Health Science
Towson University

Over the past three decades, Dr. Buchbinder has worked in many aspects of health care as a clinician, researcher, association executive, and academic. With a PhD in Public Health from the University of Illinois School of Public Health, she brings this blend of real-world experience and theoretical constructs to undergraduate and graduate face-to-face and online classrooms, where she is constantly reminded of how important good teaching really is. She also conducts healthcare management research and provides relevant and effective service to her department, college, university, and discipline, and is immediate past chair of the board of the Association of University Programs in Health Administration (AUPHA).

Jon M. Thompson, PhD

Professor and Director
Health Services Administration Program
James Madison University

Dr. Thompson holds his PhD in Health Services Organization and Research from the Medical College of Virginia/Virginia Commonwealth University. He has significant experience as a practitioner, having served as a marketing and public relations administrator at a large, hospital-based health system, and as a consultant to various health services organizations. He is an active researcher, and has published widely and presented at national meetings on diverse administrative subjects including managed care, quality, hospital operational and financial performance, human resources and healthcare teams, and healthcare marketing. In addition, he has held leadership roles in several national professional health services organizations. He has taught at both the undergraduate and graduate level in healthcare management.

Acknowledgments

This book is a result of a 14-month process involving 42 healthcare managers across 18 major healthcare settings. It has been a privilege and honor to work with each and every one of them: Larry M. Beck, Michael C. Boblitz, Sandy Cave, Stephanie Chisolm, Kristi Donovan, Teresa L. Edwards, Christopher Fanning, Valerie Fearns, William J. Forbes, Harry Fox, Treg Fuller, Schuyler Fury, Theresa C. Honchar, Andrew Jones, J. S. Parker Jones, IV, Michael Jurgensen, Sharon E. Kelley, Mary Beth Kiser, Lauren Koontz, Jim Krauss, Amanda Llewellyn, Jerod M. Loeb, Lew Lyon, Natassja Manzanero, Karen Maust, Michael J. McDonnell, Matt Neiswanger, Ryan Novak, Ryan Papa, Reena Patel, Justine Powell, Jeff Richardson, Andrea Saevoon, Jennifer R. Shapiro, Sunil K. Sinha, Justin E. Skinner, Wes Street, Richard J. Stull, Jeanine Tyler, Jennifer Villani, Jason Vollmer, and Tanisha Woodard. We are deeply grateful to these practitioners who contributed time, energy, and expertise and allowed us to use their profiles in this book. We would also like to thank our alumni, Yvonne Asante and David Eldracher, for allowing us to use their résumés as models.

Also, we would like to recognize Janel Quinn for her research assistance for this book.

And, finally, and never too often, we thank our spouses, Dale Buchbinder and Suzanne Gilchrist-Thompson, who listened to long telephone conversations about the book's progress, and tolerated our late-night and weekend hours on the computer, frantic e-mails, and faxes. We love you and could not have done this without you.

CHAPTER 1

The Healthcare Management Workforce

If you are reading this book, you are probably trying to determine what you want to do with your career and where the best jobs will be in the next 5 to 10 years. Maybe you've had family, friends, teachers, and guidance counselors pepper you with questions about your life after graduation, usually couched in phrases that begin with, "Well, when I was your age . . . ." or "You know there are a lot of jobs out there in . . . ." Perhaps you've been watching the news, and you realize that health care is a field with growing demand and a wide variety of job opportunities. Possibly you're a business person and want to apply your knowledge and skills to a different sector. Maybe you already work in a healthcare organization and wonder how you can move into a management role. Or, perhaps you're a clinician, who has spent years in direct patient care, and want to become an administrator. Whatever your educational background, age, or career level, you want to get up in the morning, go to work, be glad you are there, and *make a difference*. Job satisfaction is one thing that money cannot buy. It comes from within and is "a pleasurable or positive emotional state resulting from the appraisal of one's job or job experiences" (Locke, 1983, p. 1300). If you have vivid memories of specific work experiences, they are more likely than not to be of very good or very bad times. What you want to do is to learn to make wise career choices, minimize those bad experiences, and grow from the challenging ones. By reading this book, you will

1

have a good idea of whether this is the field for you and if you will be satisfied with the work expected of a healthcare manager.

WHY CHOOSE HEALTHCARE MANAGEMENT?

The purpose of this book is to provide an opportunity for students or professionals not familiar with the field to understand the specifics of healthcare management employment, types of available positions and career opportunities, career tracks for healthcare managers, the day-to-day responsibilities associated with these positions, and the specific challenges faced by these administrators on a daily basis. Just to tantalize you with a preview of what's ahead, here are some great reasons for choosing this field:

1. Healthcare management is one of the fastest growing career fields in the United States.
2. Healthcare management is an exciting field with opportunities for advancement.
3. There will *always* be a need for health care and healthcare managers.
4. Healthcare management offers a variety of jobs and settings, from hospitals to nursing homes to consulting firms and more.
5. Healthcare managers can help populations of people or they can help one person at a time.
6. Students learn about health care and business, making them more competitive when looking for jobs or graduate schools.
7. Practical internships and residencies enable students to get a head start in real-world experiences and jobs.
8. Most undergraduate programs have small classes, so students are able to develop personal relationships with teachers and classmates.
9. Alumni are often involved in undergraduate programs and help students to network and find jobs.
10. According to the U.S. Bureau of Labor Statistics, the average entry-to-mid-level salary for Healthcare Management graduates with a bachelor's degree is $32,000–35,000, and people with master's degrees and many years of experience can earn six-figure incomes (U.S. Bureau of Labor Statistics [BLS], 2007a).

THE ORIGINS OF HEALTHCARE MANAGEMENT

The University of Chicago founded the first program in Health Administration in 1934 under the leadership of Michael M. Davis, who had a PhD in Sociology. Davis recognized that there was no formal training for hospital managers and that an interdisciplinary program of education was needed. Envisioning the role of the healthcare manager as both a business and social role, he utilized the expertise of medical administration, social service administration, and business faculty to create an interdisciplinary model that has been replicated repeatedly across the United States and throughout the world (University of Chicago, n.d.). Originally, schools that offered a degree in Healthcare Management or Health Services Administration were all master's degree programs, geared to preparing hospital administrators. Now, in addition to master's degrees, there are baccalaureate and doctoral programs in Healthcare Management. Today, more jobs in healthcare management are being created outside of hospital settings than within. Increasing specialization of health care, burgeoning allied healthcare disciplines, a diversity of healthcare organizations, greater variety in jobs, higher expectations for healthcare outcomes, and demanding consumers mean healthcare organizations must be able to respond appropriately, effectively, and efficiently.

GROWTH AND OPPORTUNITIES

The healthcare management profession has experienced significant growth in the past 20 years. Twelve percent, or more than 1 out of every 10 working persons in the United States is employed in health care, and the salaries and demand for healthcare and social assistance workers are expected to grow by more than 25% according to the BLS (BLS, 2007a). This percentage growth is expected to be "above average" when compared to all occupations, and opportunities are expected to be especially attractive in physician practices, hospitals, home healthcare services, and outpatient care centers, according to the BLS projections. The net increase in the number of medical and health services managers needed by 2014 is forecast to be 105,000. This growth is fueled in part by the expansion in the number of direct care health organizations and healthcare-related organizations, such as ambulatory care organizations, managed care organizations, retirement communities, and assisted living firms, among others (Thompson, 2007). Hospitals will continue to employ a large number of workers; however, the rate of growth in that part of the healthcare sector will slow due to health care moving to other settings. Physicians and other healthcare practitioners will be the fastest growing employers of healthcare managers between 2006 and 2016 (BLS, 2007b).

And if those projections don't entice you to run right out and find a job in healthcare management and if you're tired of being bossed around by others, think of this: With experience, education, and the right people skills, *you* can be the boss. Opportunities for advancement in healthcare management exist in every setting. Increased demand and new managerial positions are needed to staff these organizations coupled with increased turnover as baby boomers, now entering the retirement phase of their lives, are creating rapid advancement opportunities for healthcare managers in the right place at the right time (Health Resources and Services Administration [HRSA], 2003).

While both of these important trends have created significant opportunities for health services managers, they have also raised important concerns about talent identification, recruitment, retention, and succession planning. Whereas talent scouts were once considered the purview of acting and sports, headhunters and management recruiters are looking for gifted managers with the knowledge, skills, and abilities to guide healthcare organizations through the tsunami of change in health care. Are you up to the task? Think you might be the next healthcare superstar? Take a few minutes and use the following checklist (see Table 1-1) to determine your Healthcare Management Talent Quotient!

Table 1-1   Healthcare Management Talent Quotient Quiz

Instructions: Using a scale of 1–4, where 1 = Strongly Disagree and 4 = Strongly Agree, indicate how strongly you agree or disagree with each of the following sentences regarding your knowledge, skills, and abilities. Strongly Disagree = 1 point; Disagree = 2 points; Agree = 3 points; and Strongly Agree = 4 points. Add up your total number of points to determine your Healthcare Management Talent Quotient score.

	Strongly Disagree	Disagree	Agree	Strongly Agree
I learn better by doing something.				
People tell me I am a good listener.				
I've always been interested in numbers and math.				
When I read, I readily comprehend and retain information.				
People tell me I am a good public speaker.				
I enjoy writing and look for ways to improve my writing.				
I always try to look at many sides of a question.				
I have learned how to study and improve my learning.				
Doing my best is very important to me.				
Family and friends often put me in charge of events.				
I like teaching other people new knowledge and skills.				
I am a good negotiator.				
I can be very persuasive when I need or want to be.				

Table 1-1   *Continued*

	Strongly Disagree	Disagree	Agree	Strongly Agree
I rarely lose my temper.				
I enjoy learning about other cultures.				
I enjoy being on a team and teamwork.				
I am able to communicate effectively with people from diverse cultural backgrounds.				
Men and women should have equal pay for equal work.				
I like helping people.				
I am concerned about poor, elderly, and sick people.				
The bigger the problem, the more I enjoy solving it.				
Men and women have different approaches to problem-solving.				
I like to brainstorm ideas with friends or family.				
Planning a project/event is almost as much fun as doing it.				
I like to reflect on how a project could have been improved.				
I enjoy doing research and gathering information.				
I'm good at organizing information.				
I try to identify the cause(s) of problems.				
Combining information into something new is enjoyable.				

	Strongly Disagree	Disagree	Agree	Strongly Agree
I like seeing the "big picture," i.e., how does what I'm doing fit into the community.				
I always try to do the right thing for the right reasons.				
My personal integrity is very important to me.				
Time management is very important to me.				
Money management is critical to making sure I can continue to do the things I want and need to do.				
People are the most important asset in an organization.				
I have been told I have good judgment.				

How did you score? The higher your score, the more likely you are to do well in healthcare management. This quiz is not intended to dissuade you if you have a low score. It is intended to help you to identify your aptitude at working in a healthcare setting. Fear not, these skills *can* be learned. The rest of this chapter provides an overview of what knowledge, skills, and abilities are important for you to acquire and why they are significant in healthcare management.

KNOWLEDGE BASE REQUIRED FOR HEALTHCARE MANAGEMENT

At the undergraduate level, the Association of University Programs in Health Administration (Association of University Programs in Health Administration [AUPHA], n.d.a) at www.aupha.org sets the standards for excellence in healthcare management education and encourages healthcare management (HCMN) programs to demonstrate excellence in research, practice, and educational curriculum. At the graduate level, the Commission on Accreditation of Healthcare Management Education (CAHME) does the same and "assures the highest quality educational product" (Commission on Accreditation of Healthcare Management Education [CAHME], 2007). In the following sections of this chapter, we will discuss the knowledge areas that should be covered in Healthcare Management programs. The curriculum for HCMN incorporates a multidisciplinary approach including public health, health services research, and finance and management as well as sociological, political, and economic orientations. Graduates of HCMN programs must possess the knowledge and skills necessary to enhance the management and delivery of health services and to serve as future leaders for healthcare organizations in a changing healthcare market. See Appendix B for an example of a Bachelor of Science Healthcare Management (BS, HCMN) Program of Study and Appendix C for an example of a Master of Health Administration (MHA) Program of Study. In addition, you can review undergraduate programs at the AUPHA website, www.aupha.org, and graduate programs at the CAHME website, www.cahme.org.

Liberal Arts and General Education

At the undergraduate level, general education requirements are designed to help students gain essential intellectual skills and knowledge that will be important throughout their lives, not just in an occupation. These skills include successful speaking and writing, the gathering and evaluation of information, the appreciation of diverse points of view, and the ability to understand and formulate ideas and values. "Liberal arts provide students with (1) the flexibility and resourcefulness required to adapt successfully to rapid social, economic, and technological change, (2) the understanding and tolerance necessary for informed citizenship and social action, and (3) the interest and curiosity essential to the pursuit of learning throughout the whole of life" (Towson University, 2008).

A solid HCMN curriculum integrates the liberal arts general education requirements of communication (written and oral); computational skills (mathematics and quantification); critical thinking (ability to analyze problems); and societal context (historical, philosophical, social, economic, political, and scientific foundations) with its curriculum to take advantage of this foundation and to build upon it with HCMN requirements (Towson University, 2008).

Conceptual, Technical, and Functional Competency in Management

At both the undergraduate and graduate levels, healthcare managers derive skills and knowledge from basic management theory and practice. The following competencies should be covered in an HCMN program of study: general management and theories of management including, but not limited to, content in business, law, organizational behavior, organizational design, and strategic management. Examples of course titles that will develop these competencies include accounting, economics, business law, marketing, computer literacy, financial management, human resources management, operations analysis, management information systems, strategic planning, marketing, research methods, and statistics.

Although business courses offer a sound foundation in these competencies, a solid HCMN curriculum demands healthcare-specific conceptual and technical competency in management. Students must have an understanding of the interaction of disease, public health, health promotion, and disease prevention with health, environments, organizations, populations, the healthcare delivery system, and the health professions. Examples of courses that will develop these competencies include bioethics, chronic and communicable disease, epidemiology, introduction to public health, health economics, health finance, health policy, organization of healthcare services, introduction to healthcare management, legal and ethical issues in health care, long-term administration, long-term ethical problems, and quality/performance improvement (AUPHA, n.d.b; CAHME, n.d.).

MANAGERIAL SKILLS REQUIRED FOR HEALTHCARE MANAGEMENT

Managerial skills and abilities cover a wide range of abilities including leadership, interpersonal skills, teamwork, managerial ethics, professional development, cultural competence, and motivation for continued learning.

Although leadership has always been at the forefront of people's minds when they think of managers, changes in populations, including the aging baby boomers, and ethical dilemmas are growing parts of the landscape of healthcare delivery.

For the past 30 years, the population of the United States has had dramatic changes in racial and ethnic composition (U.S. Census Bureau, 2000, 2005). In addition, the U.S. Census Bureau has projected a tripling of Hispanic and Asian populations in the next 50 years (U.S. Census Bureau, 2004). However, according to Loden and Rosener (1991, p. 20), dimensions of diversity are not limited to race and ethnicity, but also include "geography, military background, work experience, family socioeconomic status, religion, primary language, communication, learning and work styles, educational background, age, gender, physical/mental/emotional characteristics, and sexual orientation." The diversity of the populations served in health care has not yet been matched by the diversity of healthcare providers, so opportunities in healthcare management abound for students who speak a second language and are interested in and sensitive to other cultures.

Oftentimes, healthcare managers have been portrayed in the media as individuals who are only interested in the bottom line and in how much money they can make for themselves. Unfortunately, there have been occasions when greed, avarice, and access to money have tempted healthcare executives with scandals and tarnished images as the resultant outcomes. However, the American College of Healthcare Executives (ACHE) has a code of ethics that explicitly lists the behaviors expected of an ethical healthcare manager: responsibilities to the profession, patients, organization, employees, community, and society (American College of Healthcare Executives [ACHE], n.d.). Solid healthcare management programs address these issues in their curriculum at all levels—undergraduate, graduate, and executive—and cull out those students who do not act in a manner consistent with this code of ethics.

In addition, professors and employers are increasingly mindful of the need for professional demeanor and are weeding out unfit future healthcare managers. Classroom disruptions in the form of temper tantrums or "desk rage" over grades, bullying behavior toward other students, and attempts to intimidate faculty and staff are unacceptable. Students who behave in this manner will, more likely than not, be referred to the university's judicial affairs department of student affairs. If a student is not responsive to the requirements for civility training and/or anger management, then he or she does not belong in a healthcare organization. Each time you have a choice to make, you should ask yourself, "Is this ethical? Would it withstand the headline test?" If you cannot say yes, you shouldn't do it (Buchbinder, 2008, p. 2).

As Buchbinder and Thompson wrote in 2007, ". . . in healthcare management, from the day you enter the door of your first job, you will be part of an interdisciplinary team. Teamwork requires leadership, strategic thinking, diverse groups of people with different perspectives and disciplines, excellent organizational and interpersonal skills, and a good sense of humor" (p. 303). Teamwork is one of the most important competencies a healthcare manager can have and in high-quality HCMN programs, teamwork is integrated throughout the curriculum; students are required to develop the ability to work productively with a diverse, interdisciplinary team. In addition to being a good team player, the excellent healthcare manager will go above the call of duty to ensure that the organizational goals are achieved. If you are a clock-watcher and are not interested in putting in extra hours to ensure a quality product or service, healthcare management is not for you. Health care is a 24/7 business; people become ill and require services at any hour—day or night—and healthcare managers must be willing to put the patient's needs first. Like nursing and medicine, healthcare management is a sacred calling and you must be prepared to defer your own immediate gratification to work in a patient-centered organization.

Motivation for continued learning must be a priority for healthcare managers and those who choose to work in the discipline. Health care is a dynamic field; you need only to read the headlines on the Internet, in the newspapers, or to watch the evening news to realize that this is a constantly evolving field. If you are not interested in lifelong learning, then healthcare management is not the right choice for you. For example, the American College of Healthcare Executives offers postgraduate credentialing. Board certification as a Fellow in the American College of Healthcare Executives (FACHE) is a demonstration of one's commitment to the field and provides opportunities for advancement and professional growth (ACHE, n.d.). Other professional organizations, such as the Medical Group Management Association (MGMA) and the American College of Health Care Administrators (ACHCA), also offer certification programs for healthcare management professionals.

EXPERIENTIAL LEARNING REQUIRED FOR HEALTHCARE MANAGEMENT

David Kolb's experiential learning cycle model states that learning is the process and knowledge is the outcome; learning becomes knowledge when the learner is caught up in the experience (Kolb, 1984). Kolb argued that the most meaningful learning, knowledge acquisition, and integration occur when the learner progresses through all four stages of Abstract Conceptualization, Active Experimentation, Concrete Experience, and Reflective Observation. Another researcher, Donald Schön, called the phenomenon of learning through experience, "knowing-in-action," which becomes "knowledge-in-action" (Schön, 1983, p. 59). He argued that practitioners "know-in-doing" and that their art could be taught to others. In his subsequent work (1987), Schön indicated that real-world problems are not clean, pristine, and textbook perfect. They are messy, overwhelming, and full of underlying themes, issues, and agendas that may not be related to the practitioner's discipline, but influence the problem at hand. Practitioners name and identify what is relevant and create a conceptual framework for problem solving according to their training and discipline (Buchbinder et al., 2005). To succeed in practice, healthcare managers must be able to wrangle their way through these tricky problems.

In addition to issues related to cost, quality, and access, real-world healthcare management problems are tangled up in personalities and politics. Healthcare employers are looking for people who are team players, problem solvers, and politically savvy self-starters, who will go above the call of duty. Solid healthcare management programs utilize a wide variety of approaches to develop the knowledge, skills, and abilities needed for this fluid environment. In addition to the traditional readings, quizzes, examinations, and research papers, educators in healthcare management also utilize self-assessment tools, reflective papers, online discussions, in-class lectures and discussion, case studies, and role play.

Experiential learning, such as case studies focused on healthcare settings and extensive teamwork, group projects, team and individual presentations, role play, and internships, are signature teaching methods in most HCMN curricula. Faculty-supervised internships, practica, and projects in healthcare organizations provide an opportunity for students to learn how to apply theory and principles in the context of work situations and to develop skills essential to these tasks. In addition to providing an opportunity for the transition from the student to professional role, at the under-graduate level internships offer the chance to try out a job without risk. If it turns out that it was something you never want to do again, you have gained that knowledge without looking like a job-hopper after you graduate.

Internships give you opportunities for networking, to find a mentor, and to see what kinds of roles exist. Also, internships allow you to practice what you have learned by demonstrating your knowledge and skills, and help to further develop your competencies (Thompson, 2005). Many healthcare management graduates obtain their first job from their internship. Internships should be treated like a very long job interview: Every day is a chance for the intern to demonstrate how indispensible he or she can be to the organization. Healthcare management interns are welcomed enthusiastically by health services organization practitioners. The most frequent question posed preceptors at the end of an internship placement is "When can we have another intern?" Likewise, undergraduate students always say the internship is the most useful part of the curriculum. At the graduate level, many universities offer a paid administrative residency or practicum, that is, eight-months to one-year-long training with a health-care executive preceptor who has made the commitment to mentor and coach a student into an executive role. As Xavier University notes, these experiential educational opportunities provide you with "intensive project and management experiences . . . invaluable for developing a strong management foundation and helping you launch a successful career" (Xavier University, 2008).

CHAPTER SUMMARY

Healthcare management is one of the fastest growing fields in the United States. Opportunities for employment and a satisfying career are expected to be above average for the next two decades. Critical learning includes: liberal arts; conceptual, technical, and functional competency in general management and healthcare management; managerial skills and abilities; and experiential learning where you can apply classroom theory to real-world healthcare management. If you are willing to study and work hard, the dynamic field of healthcare management might just be the career for you.

REFERENCES

American College of Healthcare Executives. (n.d.). *ACHE code of ethics*. Retrieved July 22, 2008, from http://www.ache.org/ABT_ACHE/code.cfm

American College of Healthcare Executives. (n.d.). *FACHE: Advancement to fellow*. Retrieved July 22, 2008, from http://www.ache.org/mbership/credentialing/credentialing.cfm

Association of University Programs in Health Administration. (n.d.a). *Program certification and accreditation*. Retrieved November 18, 2008, from http://www.aupha.org/i4a/pages/index.crm?pageid=3518

Association of University Programs in Health Administration (n.d.b). *Criteria for undergraduate program certification*. Retrieved November 18, 2008, from http://www.aupha.org/files/public/2008++%20UNDERGRADUATE%20CRITERIA.pdf

Buchbinder, S. B. (2008, Spring). Walking the talk. *AUPHA Exchange*, p. 2.

Buchbinder, S. B., Alt, P. M., Eskow, K., Forbes, W., Hester, E., Struck, M., et al. (2005, June). Creating learning prisms with an interdisciplinary case study workshop. *Innovative Higher Education, 29*(4). Retrieved July 22, 2008, from http://www.springerlink.com/content/h8k6k2537l603h04/

Buchbinder, S. B., & Thompson, J. M. (2007). Teamwork. In S. B. Buchbinder & N. H. Shanks (Eds.), *Introduction to health care management* (p. 303). Sudbury, MA: Jones and Bartlett.

Commission on Accreditation of Healthcare Management Education. (n.d.). *About CAHME: Historical overview*. Retrieved November 18, 2008, from http://cahme.org/History.html

Health Resources and Services Administration. (2003, Spring). *Changing demographics: Implications for physicians, nurses, and other health workers*. United States Department of Health and Human Services, Health Resources and Services Administration, Bureau of Health Professions, National Center for Health Workforce Analysis. Retrieved July 22, 2008, from http://bhpr.hrsa.gov/healthworkforce/reports/changedemo/content.htm

Kolb, D. A. (1984). *Experiential learning: Experience as the source of learning and development*. Englewood Cliffs, NJ: Prentice-Hall.

Locke, E. A. (1983). The nature and causes of job satisfaction. In M. Dunnette (Ed.), *Handbook of industrial and organizational psychology* (pp. 1297–1349). New York: John Wiley and Sons.

Loden, M., & Rosener, J. B. (1991). *Workforce America! Managing employee diversity as a vital resource*. Homewood, IL: Business One Irwin.

Schön, D. A. (1983). *The reflective practitioner: How professionals think in action*. New York: Basic Books.

Schön, D. A. (1987). *Educating the reflective practitioner*. San Francisco: Jossey-Bass.

Thompson, J. M. (2005, Fall). Competency development and assessment in undergraduate healthcare management programs: The role of internships. *The Journal of Health Administration Education, 22*, 417–433.

Thompson, J. M. (2007). Health services administration. In S. Chisolm (Ed.), *The health professions: Trends and opportunities in U.S. health care* (pp. 357–372). Sudbury, MA: Jones and Bartlett.

Towson University. (2008). *General education requirements.* Retrieved July 22, 2008, from http://www.towson.edu/registrar/Degree/geneds/index.asp

U.S. Bureau of Labor Statistics. (2007a, Fall). *Occupational outlook quarterly.* Retrieved July 22, 2008, from http://www.bls.gov/opub/ooq/2007/fall/art03.pdf

U.S. Bureau of Labor Statistics. (2007b, December). *Occupational outlook handbook, 2008–2009 Edition.* Medical and Health Services Managers. Retrieved July 22, 2008, from http://www.bls.gov/oco/ocos014.htm

U.S. Census Bureau. (2000). *Census 2000 demographic profile highlights.* Retrieved July 22, 2008, from http://factfinder.census.gov/servlet/ACSSAFFFacts?_event=&geo_id=01000US&_geoContext=01000US&_street=&_county=&_cityTown=&_state=&_zip=&_lang=en&_sse=on&ActiveGeoDiv=&_useEV=&pctxt=fph&pgsl=010&_submenuId=factsheet_1&ds_name=DEC_2000_SAFF&_ci_nbr=null&qr_name=null&reg=null%3Anull&_keyword=&_industry=

U.S. Census Bureau. (2004). *Census bureau projects tripling of Hispanic and Asian populations in 50 years; non-Hispanic whites may drop to half of total population.* Retrieved July 22, 2008, from http://www.census.gov/Press-Release/www/releases/archives/population/001720.html

U.S. Census Bureau. (2005). *2006 American community survey data profile highlights.* Retrieved July 22, 2008, from http://factfinder.census.gov/servlet/ACSSAFFFacts?_event=&geo_id=01000US&_geoContext=01000US&_street=&_county=&_cityTown=&_state=&_zip=&_lang=en&_sse=on&ActiveGeoDiv=&_useEV=&pctxt=fph&pgsl=010&_submenuId=factsheet_1&ds_name=DEC_2000_SAFF&_ci_nbr=null&qr_name=null&reg=null%3Anull&_keyword=&_industry=

University of Chicago, School of Social Service Administration, Chicago, IL. The graduate program in health administration and policy. (n.d.). *About GPHAP.* Retrieved July 22, 2008, from http://gphap.uchicago.edu/aboutgphap.shtml

Xavier University. (2008). *Residency.* Retrieved November 18, 2008, from http://www.xavier.edu/mhsa/Residency.cfm

CHAPTER 2

Understanding Healthcare Management

The prior chapter addressed growth in the health services industry and opportunities for healthcare managers. By now the reader should appreciate that formal preparation in healthcare management can pay big dividends in terms of exciting management jobs and positions with excellent career advancement. But just what do healthcare managers do? And what are their roles and responsibilities?

Healthcare management is the profession that provides leadership and direction to organizations that deliver personal health services, and to divisions, departments, units, or services within those organizations. This chapter gives a comprehensive overview of healthcare management as a profession. Understanding the roles, responsibilities, and functions carried out by healthcare managers is important for those individuals considering the field to make informed decisions about the "fit." This chapter provides a discussion of key management roles, responsibilities, and functions, as well as management positions at different levels within healthcare organizations. In addition, descriptions of supervisory level, mid-level, and senior management positions within different organizations are provided.

THE NEED FOR MANAGEMENT AND THEIR PERSPECTIVE

Healthcare organizations are complex and dynamic. The nature of organizations requires that managers provide leadership, as well as the supervision and coordination of employees. Organizations were created to achieve goals that were beyond the capacity of any single individual. In healthcare organizations, the scope and complexity of tasks carried out in provision of services are so great that individual staff operating on their own couldn't get the job done. Moreover, the necessary tasks in producing services in healthcare organizations require the coordination of many highly specialized disciplines that must work together seamlessly. Managers are needed to make certain that organizational tasks are carried out in the best way possible to achieve organizational goals and that appropriate resources, including financial and human resources, are adequate to support the organization.

Healthcare managers are appointed to positions of authority where they shape the organization by making important decisions. Such decisions, for example, relate to recruitment and development of staff, acquisition of technology, service additions and reductions, and allocation and spending of financial resources. Decisions made by healthcare managers not only focus on ensuring that the patient receives the most appropriate, timely, and effective services possible, but also address achievement of performance targets that are desired by the manager. Ultimately, decisions made by an individual manager affect the organization's overall performance.

Managers must consider two domains as they carry out various tasks and make decisions (Thompson, 2007a). These domains are termed **external** and **internal domains** (see Table 2-1). The **external domain** refers to the influences, resources, and activities that exist outside the boundary of the organization but which significantly affect the organization. These factors include community needs, population characteristics, and reimbursement from commercial insurers and Medicare and Medicaid. The **internal domain** refers to those areas of focus that managers need to address on a daily basis, such as ensuring the appropriate number and types of staff, financial performance, and quality of care. These internal areas reflect the operation of the organization where the manager has the most control. Keeping the dual perspective requires significant balance on the part of management and significant effort in order to make good decisions.

Table 2-1   Domains of Health Services Administration

External	Internal
Community Demographics/Need	Staffing
Licensure	Budgeting
Accreditation	Quality services
Regulations	Patient satisfaction
Stakeholder Demands	Physician relations
Competitors	Financial performance
Medicare and Medicaid	Technology acquisition
Managed care organizations/Insurers	New service development

Source: J.M. Thompson, "Health Services Administration" in S. Chisolm (Ed.), *The Health Professions: Trends and Opportunities in U.S. Health Care*, 2007.

MANAGEMENT: DEFINITION, FUNCTIONS, AND COMPETENCIES

As discussed earlier, management is needed to support and coordinate the services that are provided within healthcare organizations. Management has been defined as the process, comprised of social and technical functions and activities, occurring within organizations for the purpose of accomplishing predetermined objectives through humans and other resources (Longest, Rakich, & Darr, 2000). Implicit in the definition is that managers work through and with other people, carrying out technical and interpersonal activities, in order to achieve desired objectives of the organization. Others have stated that a manager is anyone in the organization who supports and is responsible for the work performance of one or more other persons (Lombardi & Schermerhorn, 2007).

While most beginning students of healthcare management tend to focus on the role of the senior manager or lead administrator of an organization, it should be realized that management occurs through many others who may not have "manager" in their position title. Examples of some of these managerial positions in healthcare organizations include supervisor, coordinator, and director, among others (see Table 2-2). These levels of managerial control are discussed in more detail in the next section.

Table 2-2   Managerial Positions, By Organizational Setting

Organizational Setting	Examples of Managerial Positions
Physician Practice	Practice Manager Director of Medical Records Supervisor, Billing Office
Nursing Home	Administrator Manager, Business Office Director, Food Services Admissions Coordinator Supervisor, Environmental Services
Hospital	Chief Executive Officer Vice President, Marketing Clinical Nurse Manager Director, Revenue Management Supervisor, Maintenance

Managers implement six management functions as they carry out the process of management (Longest, Rakich, & Darr, 2000):

Planning: This function requires the manager to set a direction and determine what needs to be accomplished. It means setting priorities and determining performance targets.

Organizing: This management function refers to the overall design of the organization or the specific division, unit, or service for which the manager is responsible. Further, it means designating reporting relationships and intentional patterns of interaction. Determining positions, teamwork assignments, and distribution of authority and responsibility are critical components of this function.

Staffing: This function refers to acquiring and retaining human resources. It also refers to developing and maintaining the workforce through various strategies and tactics.

Controlling: This function refers to monitoring staff activities and performance, and taking the appropriate actions for corrective action to increase performance.

Directing: The focus in this function is on initiating action in the organization through effective leadership and motivation of, and communication with, subordinates.

Decision making: This function is critical to all of the aforementioned management functions and means making effective decisions based on consideration of benefits and the drawbacks of alternatives.

In order to effectively carry out these functions, the manager needs to possess several key competencies. Katz (1974) identified several key competencies of the effective manager, including conceptual, technical, and interpersonal skills. The term **competency** refers to a state in which an individual has the requisite or adequate ability or qualities to perform certain functions (Ross, Wenzel, & Mitlying, 2002). These are defined as follows:

Conceptual skills are those skills that involve the ability to critically analyze and solve complex problems. Examples: a manager conducts an analysis of the best way to provide a service, or determines a strategy to reduce patient complaints regarding food service.

Technical skills are those skills that reflect expertise or ability to perform a specific work task. Examples: a manager develops and implements a new incentive compensation program for staff or designs and implements modifications to a computer-based staffing model.

Interpersonal skills are those skills that enable a manager to communicate with and work well with other individuals, regardless of whether they are peers, supervisors, or subordinates. Examples: a manager counsels an employee whose performance is below expectation, or communicates to subordinates the desired performance level for a service for the next fiscal year.

MANAGEMENT POSITIONS: THE CONTROL IN THE ORGANIZATIONAL HIERARCHY

Management positions within healthcare organizations are not confined to the top level; because of the size and complexity of many healthcare organizations, management positions are found throughout the organization. Management positions exist at lower levels, middle-management levels, and at upper levels, which is referred to as senior management level. The hierarchy of management means that authority, or power, is delegated downward in the organization, and that lower-level managers have less authority than higher-level managers whose scope of responsibility is much greater. For example, a vice president of Patient Care Services in a hospital may be in charge of several different functional areas, such as nursing, diagnostic imaging services, and laboratory services; in contrast, a director of Medical Records—a lower-level position—has responsibility only for the function of patient medical records. Furthermore, a supervisor within the Environmental Services department may have responsibility for only a small housekeeping staff, whose work is critical, but confined to a defined area of the organization. Some managerial positions, such as those discussed above, are **line** managerial positions because the manager supervises other employees; other managerial positions are **staff** managerial positions because they carry out work and advise their boss, but they do not routinely supervise others. Managerial positions also vary in terms of required expertise and or experience; some positions require extensive knowledge of many substantive areas and significant working experience, and other positions are more appropriate for entry level managers who have limited or no experience.

The most common organizational structure for healthcare organizations is a **functional organizational structure** whose key characteristic is a pyramid-shaped hierarchy, which defines the functions carried out and the key management positions assigned to those functions (see Figure 2-1). The size and complexity of the specific health services organization will dictate the particular structure. For example, larger organizations—such as large community hospitals, hospital systems, and academic medical centers—will likely have deep vertical structures reflecting varying levels of administrative control for the organization. This structure is necessary due to the large scope of services provided and the corresponding vast array of administrative and support services that are needed to enable the delivery of clinical services. Other characteristics associated with this functional structure include a strict chain of command and line of reporting, which ensures that communication and assignment and evaluation of tasks are carried out in a linear **command and control** environment. This structure offers key advantages, such as specific divisions of labor and clear lines of reporting and accountability.

Other administrative structures have been adopted by healthcare organizations, usually in combination with a functional structure. These include **matrix** or **team-based models** and **service line management models**. The **matrix model** recognizes that a strict functional structure may limit the

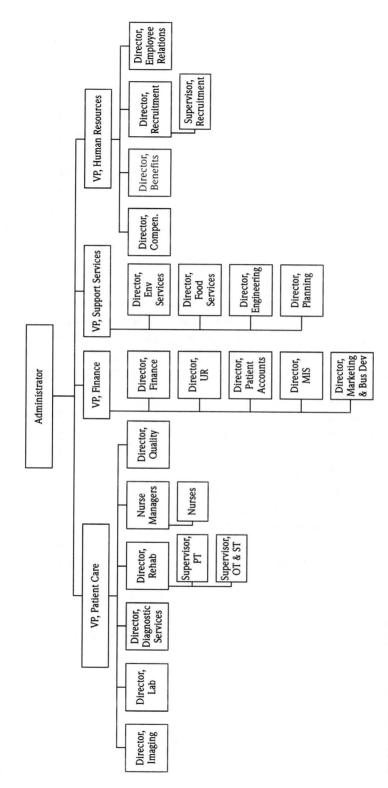

FIGURE 2-1 Functional Organizational Structure

organization's flexibility to carry out the work, and that the expertise of other disciplines is needed on a continuous basis. An example of the matrix method is when functional staff, such as nursing and rehabilitation personnel, are assigned to a specific program such as geriatrics and they report for programmatic purposes to the program director of the Geriatrics department. Another example is when clinical staff and administrative staff are assigned to a team investigating new services that is headed by a marketing or business development manager. In both of these examples, management would lead staff who traditionally are not under their direct administrative control. Advantages of this structure include improved lateral communication and coordination of services, as well as pooled knowledge.

In **service line management**, a manager is appointed to head a specific clinical service line and has responsibility and accountability for staffing, resource acquisition, budget, and financial control associated with the array of services provided under that service line. Typical examples of service lines include cardiology, oncology (cancer), women's services, physical rehabilitation, and behavioral health (mental health). Service lines can be established within a single organization, or may cut across affiliated organizations such as within a hospital system where services are provided at several different affiliated facilities (Boblitz & Thompson, 2005). Some facilities have found that the service line management model for selected clinical services has resulted in many benefits, such as lower costs, higher quality of care, and greater patient satisfaction compared to other management models (Duffy & Lemieux, 1995). The service line management model is usually implemented within an organization in conjunction with a functional structure, as the organization may choose to give special emphasis and additional resources to one or a few services lines.

FOCUS OF MANAGEMENT: SELF, UNIT/TEAM, AND ORGANIZATION

Effective healthcare management involves exercising professional judgment and skills and carrying out the aforementioned managerial functions at three levels: self, unit/team, and organization wide. First and foremost, the individual manager must be able to **effectively manage himself or herself**. This means managing time, information, space, and materials; being responsive and following through with peers, supervisors, and clients; maintaining a positive attitude and high motivation; and keeping understanding of management techniques and substantive issues of health-care management current. Managing yourself also means developing and applying appropriate technical, interpersonal, and conceptual skills and competences and being comfortable with them, in order to be able to effectively move to the next level—that of supervising others.

The second focus of management is the **unit/team work level**. The expertise of the manager at this level involves managing others in terms of effectively completing the work. Regardless of whether you are a senior manager, mid-level manager, or supervisor, you will be "supervising" others as expected in your assigned role. This responsibility includes assigning work tasks, review and modification of assignments, monitoring and review of individual performance, and carrying out the management functions described earlier to ensure excellent delivery of services. This focal area is where the actual work gets done. Performance reflects the interaction of the manager and the employee, and it is incumbent on the manager to do what is needed to shape the performance of individual employees at this level.

The third management focus is at the **organizational level**. This focal area reflects the fact that managers must work together as part of the larger organization to ensure organizational-level performance and organizational viability. In other words, the success of the organization depends upon the success of its individual parts, and effective collaboration is needed to ensure that this occurs. The range of clinical and nonclinical activities that occur within a healthcare organization requires that managers who head individual units work closely with other unit managers to provide services. Sharing of information, collaboration, and communication are essential for success. The hierarchy looks to the contribution of each supervised unit as it pertains to the whole. Individual managers' contributions to the overall performance of the organization—in terms of various performance measures such as cost, quality, satisfaction, and access—are important and measured.

ROLE OF THE MANAGER IN TALENT MANAGEMENT

In order to effectively master the focal areas of management and carry out the required management functions, management must have the requisite number and types of highly motivated employees. From a strategic perspective, healthcare organizations compete for labor, and it is commonly accepted today that high-performing healthcare organizations are dependent upon individual human performance (Thompson, 2007b). Many observers have advocated for healthcare organizations to view their employees as strategic assets who can create a competitive advantage (Becker, Huselid, & Ulrich, 2001). Therefore, human resources management has been replaced in many healthcare organizations with "talent management." The focus has shifted to securing and retaining the talent needed to do the job in the best way, rather than simply fill a role (Huselid, Beatty, & Becker, 2005).

Beyond recruitment, managers are concerned about developing and retaining those staff who are excellent performers. There are several strategies used by managers to create and maintain excellent performers. These include formal methods such as offering training programs, assisting with hands-on leadership, providing continuing education, especially for clinical and technical fields, and providing job enrichment. In addition, managers use informal methods such as conducting periodic employee reviews, soliciting employee feedback, offering employee suggestion programs, and other methods of fostering high-involvement employee relations.

ROLE OF THE MANAGER IN ENSURING HIGH PERFORMANCE

At the end of the day, the role of the manager is to ensure that the unit, service, division, or organization he or she leads achieves **high performance**. What exactly is meant by high performance? To understand performance, one has to appreciate the value of setting and meeting goals and objectives for the unit/service and organization as a whole, in terms of the work that is being carried out. **Goals and objectives** are desired end points for activity and reflect strategic and operational directions for the organization. They are specific, measurable, meaningful, and time-oriented. Goals and objectives for individual units should reflect the overarching needs and expectations of the organization as a whole, because as the reader will recall, all entities are working together to achieve high levels of overall organizational performance.

Griffith (2000) refers to high performing organizations as being championship organizations—that is, they expect to perform well on different yet meaningful measures of performance. Griffith further defines the "championship processes" and the need to develop **performance measures** in each: governance and strategic management; clinical quality, including customer satisfaction; clinical organization (caregivers); financial planning; planning and marketing; information services; human resources; and plant and supplies. For each championship process, the organization should establish measures of desired performance that will guide the organization. Examples of measures include medication errors, surgical complications, patient satisfaction, staff turnover rates, employee satisfaction, market share, profit margin, and revenue growth, among others. In turn, respective divisions, units, and services will set targets and carry out activities to address key performance processes. The manager's job, ultimately, is to ensure that these targets are met by carrying out the previously discussed management functions. A control process for managers has been advanced by Ginter, Swayne, and Duncan (2002) that describes five key steps in the performance management process: set objectives, measure performance, compare performance with objectives, determine reasons for deviation, and take corrective action. Management's job is to ensure that performance is maintained, or, if below expectations, is improved.

Stakeholders, including insurers, state and federal governments, and consumer advocacy groups, are expecting, and in many cases demanding, acceptable levels of performance in healthcare organizations. These groups want to make sure that services are provided in a safe, convenient, low-cost, and high-quality environment. For example, the Commission (formerly JCAHO) has set minimum standards for healthcare facilities operations that ensure quality, the National Committee for Quality Assurance (NCQA) has set standards for measuring performance of health plans, and the Centers for Medicare and Medicaid Services (CMS) has established a website that compares hospital performance along a number of critical dimensions.

In addition to meeting the reporting requirements of the aforementioned organizations, many healthcare organizations today use varying methods of measuring and reporting the performance measurement process. Common methods include developing and using dashboards or balanced scorecards that allow for a quick interpretation on the performance across a number of key measures (Curtright, Stolp-Smith, & Edell, 2000; Pieper, 2005). Senior administration uses these methods to measure and communicate performance on the total organization to the governing board and other critical constituents. Other managers use these methods at the division, unit, or service level to profile its performance. In turn, these measures are also used to evaluate their performance and are considered in decisions by the manager's boss regarding compensation adjustments, promotions, increased or reduced responsibility, training and development, and, if necessary, termination or reassignment.

ROLE OF THE MANAGER IN SUCCESSION PLANNING

Due to the competitive nature of healthcare organizations and the need for highly motivated and skilled employees, managers are faced with the challenge of succession planning for their organizations. **Succession planning** refers to the concept of taking actions to ensure that staff can move up in management roles within the organization, in order to replace those managers who retire or move to other opportunities in other organizations. Succession planning has most recently been emphasized at the senior level of organizations, in part due to the large number of retirements that are anticipated from baby boomer chief executive officers (CEOs; Burt, 2005). In order to continue the emphasis on high performance within healthcare organizations, CEOs and other senior managers are interested in finding and nurturing leadership talent within their organizations who can assume the responsibility and carry forward the important work of these organizations.

Healthcare organizations are currently engaged in several practices to address leadership succession needs. First, **mentoring programs** for junior management that senior management participate in have been advocated as a good way to prepare future healthcare leaders (Rollins, 2003). Mentoring studies show that mentors view their efforts as helpful to the organization (Finley, Ivanitskaya, & Kennedy, 2007). Some observers suggest that having many mentors is essential to capturing the necessary scope of expertise, experience, interest, and contacts to maximize professional growth (Broscio & Sherer, 2003). Mentoring middle-level managers for success as they transitioned to their current positions is also helpful to preparing those managers for future executive leadership roles (Kubica, 2008).

A second method of succession planning is through **formal leadership development programs**. These programs are intended to identify management potential throughout an organization by targeting specific skill sets of individuals and assessing their match to specific jobs, such as vice president or chief operating officer (COO). One way to implement this is through talent reviews, which when done annually, help create a pool of existing staff who may be excellent candidates for further leadership development and skill strengthening through the establishment of development plans. Formal programs that are being established by many healthcare organizations focus on high-potential people (Burt, 2005).

CHAPTER SUMMARY

The profession of healthcare management is challenging and requires that persons in managerial positions at all levels of the organization possess sound conceptual, technical, and interpersonal skills in order to carry out the required managerial functions of planning, organizing, staffing, directing, controlling, and decision making. In addition, managers must maintain a dual perspective where they understand the external and internal domains of their organization, and the need for development at the self, unit/team, and organization levels. Opportunities exist for managerial talent at all levels of a healthcare organization, including supervisory, middle-management, and senior-management levels. The role of manager is critical to ensuring a high level of organizational performance, and managers are also instrumental in talent recruitment and retention as well as succession planning.

REFERENCES

Becker, B. E., Huselid, M. A., & Ulrich, D. (2001). *The HR scorecard: Linking people, strategy, and performance.* Boston: Harvard Business School Press.

Boblitz, M., & Thompson, J. M. (2005, October). Assessing the feasibility of developing centers of excellence: Six initial steps. *Healthcare Financial Management, 59,* 72–84.

Broscio, M., & Scherer, J. (2003, May/June). Building job security: Strategies for becoming a highly valued contributor. *Journal of Healthcare Management, 48,* 147–151.

Burt, T. (2005). Leadership development as a corporate strategy: Using talent reviews to improve senior management. *Healthcare Executive, 20,* 14–18.

Curtright, J. W., Stolp-Smith, S. C., & Edell, E. S. (2000). Strategic management: Development of a performance measurement system at the Mayo Clinic. *Journal of Healthcare Management, 45,* 58–68.

Duffy, J. R., & Lemieux, K. G. (1995, Fall). A cardiac service line approach to patient-centered care. *Nursing Administration Quarterly, 20,* 12–23.

Finley, F. R., Ivanitskaya, L. V., & Kennedy, M. H. (2007, July/August). Mentoring junior healthcare administrators: A description of mentoring practices in 127 U.S. hospitals. *Journal of Healthcare Management, 52,* 260–270.

Ginter, P. M., Swayne, L. E., & Duncan, W. J. (2002). *Strategic management of healthcare organizations* (4th ed.). Malden, MA: Blackwell.

Griffith, J. R. (2000, January/February). Championship management for healthcare organizations. *Journal of Healthcare Management, 45,* 17–31.

Huselid, M. A., Beatty, R. W., & Becker, B. E. (2005, December). "A players" or "A" positions? The strategic logic of workforce management. *Harvard Business Review, 83,* 100–117.

Katz, R. L. (1974, September/October). Skills of an effective administrator. *Harvard Business Review, 52,* 90–102.

Kubica, A. J. (2008, March/April). Transitioning middle managers. *Healthcare Executive, 23,* 58–60.

Lombardi, D. M., & Schermerhorn, J. R. (2007). *Healthcare management.* Hoboken, NJ: John Wiley and Sons.

Longest, B. B., Rakich, J. S., & Darr, K. (2000). *Managing health services organizations and systems.* Baltimore: Health Professions Press.

Pieper, S. K. (2005, May/June). Reading the right signals: How to strategically manage with scorecards. *Healthcare Executive, 20,* 9–14.

Rollins, G. (2003). Succession planning: Laying the foundation for smooth transitions and effective leaders. *Healthcare Executive, 18,* 14–18.

Ross, A., Wenzel, F. J., & Mityling, J. W. (2002). *Leadership for the future: Core competencies in health care.* Chicago, Illinois: Health Administration Press/AUPHA Press.

Thompson, J. M. (2007a). Health services administration. In S. Chisolm (Ed.), *The health professions: Trends and opportunities in U.S. health care* (pp. 357–372). Sudbury, MA: Jones and Bartlett.

Thompson, J. M. (2007b). The strategic management of human resources. In S. B. Buchbinder & N. H. Shanks (Eds.), *Introduction to healthcare management* (pp. 265–301). Sudbury, MA: Jones and Bartlett.

Healthcare Management Practice Settings

This chapter presents summaries of the major settings for the practice of healthcare management. Each setting summary provides information on the nature of services provided, opportunities for healthcare management careers, different types of managerial positions in these settings, key managerial skills and competencies required for the setting, challenges specific to management in the setting, and, where available, information on compensation. Salary information is recognized as hard to come by; the reader should keep in mind that salary information is presented as a guide only, and that individual healthcare manager salaries vary significantly by type and level of position; type, size, and complexity of the organization; individual education and experience; and geographic region. It is not possible to describe all settings for healthcare management; therefore, we have chosen to focus on those settings that best illustrate the range of opportunities.

UNDERSTANDING PRACTICE SETTINGS: DIRECT AND NON-DIRECT CARE

A helpful way to classify opportunities in healthcare management is to describe them as direct care settings and non-direct care settings. **Direct care settings** are those organizations that provide care directly to a patient, resident, or client who seeks services from the organization. Examples include hospitals, nursing homes, physician practices, and assisted living facilities, among others. **Non-direct care settings** are important sectors of health services. These settings are not directly involved in the provision of care to persons needing health services, but rather support the care of individuals through products and services made available to direct care settings. Examples include consulting firms, associations, pharmaceutical companies, and medical suppliers, among others.

DIRECT CARE SETTINGS

Ambulatory Care Organizations/Clinics

The term ambulatory care organization covers the wide range and variety of organizations that provide services to anyone who can ambulate, or walk, into the door and is not kept overnight at the facility. These facilities can be stand-alone or part of a hospital or hospital system, and are often seen in high-traffic areas, across the street from shopping centers, or lately, in large chain retail stores. According to Barr and Breindel (2004, p. 507), the most common types of ambulatory care facilities are:

- Urgent care or emergency care
- Outpatient diagnostics (imaging, ultrasound, blood work, electrocardiograms)
- Home care
- Outpatient surgery
- Physician care
- Outpatient radiation therapy treatment
- Outpatient infusion therapy

Opportunities for Healthcare Management Careers

Over the past two decades, more and more ambulatory services are being provided outside of hospital walls and systems. It is not uncommon for plastic surgeons to have their own operating rooms in their offices and for infertility specialists to have their own, separate *in vitro* fertilization facilities. Laser eye surgery, once provided only in hospital operating rooms, is now available in shopping malls, along with teeth whitening, and massage therapies. The reason for this dramatic shift is in large part due to better physician reimbursement by insurance companies and lower overhead costs. Physicians in freestanding facilities do not pay high hospital overhead for services that are not part of their direct costs for production of their services, such as human resources and the mail room. Opportunities for employment in these settings have grown by a third over the last decade (Barr & Breindel, 2004) and will continue to grow in the future. Some examples of managerial positions in these settings include clinic administrator/manager, ambulatory department manager I or II, marketing manager, patient administration manager, and administrative services manager.

Key Managerial Skills and Competencies Required

As noted above, these services have moved into retail settings—which means the patients have evolved into discerning healthcare consumers and customers. If you choose to work in these settings, you must know your customer and how your organization is perceived by the healthcare consumer. Is your facility a high-end boutique with expensive, self-pay cosmetic surgery? Or is it a walk-in, self-pay clinic in a chain retail store? Customer service skills are critical in these settings; patients can literally walk down the street to another urgent care setting if they are not happy with the service they are receiving. Active consumer complaints are only the tip of the iceberg. If one customer complains, that means there are 10 to 15 who are dissatisfied, but haven't bothered to complain. Unhappy customers can do real damage to a business. Complainers will tell twice as many people as will happy customers (Baer, 1996).

An excellent understanding of managing the numbers of patients and when they are seen, that is, applied queuing theory, is a key competency. If you have ever been to a theme park, you probably were informed about how long the wait would be to get on a ride. In healthcare services, and especially in these settings, you will need to be able to manage the number of patients and services provided. In some facilities, such as outpatient surgery, you can control the arrival of patients and demand for services by scheduling operations. In other settings, such as a walk-in urgent or emergency care clinic, arrivals will be random, unpredictable, and unscheduled. You will need to understand how to manage the queue by analyzing past data to provide estimates of demand for healthcare services and to staff appropriately (Seidel, Gorsky, & Lewis, 1995). If nurses and physicians are idle because the clinic is overstaffed, they are unproductive and labor costs will exceed revenues, leading to losses. Conversely, if the clinic is under-staffed and there is a long wait time to see a nurse, a nurse practitioner, a physician's assistant, or a physician, patients will become highly dissatisfied and will leave, and tell lots of people about how unhappy they are.

Challenges Specific to the Setting

Marketing your ambulatory organization and making your facility stand out in a crowd is a key challenge, along with ensuring quality of care and customer satisfaction. Accreditation of these facilities is also a key challenge and managers in these settings must be aware of the standards and criteria that apply to their facilities: Lack of accreditation can cause loss of revenues from payers such as Medicare, Medicaid, and private health insurance plans. The Joint Commission has been accrediting ambulatory care orga-nizations since 1975 (The Joint Commission, 2008), and the Accredita-tion Association for Ambulatory Health Care (AAAHC), established in 1979, has been working with ambulatory care organizations "to assist ambulatory healthcare organizations improve the quality of care provided to patients" (Accreditation Association for Ambulatory Health Care [AAAHC], 2008). With increasing emphasis on outcomes measurement, accreditation standards are foremost on everyone's agenda.

Salary and Compensation

Salaries and compensation in ambulatory care settings will vary by the size of the organization, the level of responsibility, and your experience. In 2006, according to the BLS, the median annual earnings for outpatient care facilities were $67,920 (BLS, 2007a). Keep in mind this figure does not represent an entry-level salary, but rather the range of salaries in these settings with this number at the middle of the range.

Health Departments: Local, County, State, and Federal

Public health is the application of preventive medicine at the macro-level of populations, rather than the micro-level of individuals. The goal of all public health agencies is to prevent disease and promote health and wellness. Essential or core functions of all public health agencies include "assessment or the systematic collection and analysis of available data that describe the health status of the community, the needs of the community, and other epidemiologic studies of health problems; policy development based on the level of scientific and technical knowledge and on the content of public values and popular opinions, with priorities set by the community; and assurance that the agreed-upon goals are being met" (Sharrar, 1992, p. 2).

The Department of Health and Human Services is "the U.S. government's principal agency for protecting the health of all Americans and providing essential human services, especially for those who are least able to help themselves" (U.S. Department of Health and Human Services [HHS], 2008a). Through hundreds of agencies, including the world famous National Institutes of Health, with thousands of employees, HHS works with state, local, and county governments to ensure the health and wellness of U.S. citizens. Most of these federal agencies have headquarters in or around Washington, DC, with the exception of the Centers for Disease Control and Prevention (CDC) in Atlanta, Georgia.

State governments assess state-level health needs, establish state health objectives, conduct statewide planning with input from city and county public health officials, ensure a minimum standard of essential health services, and monitor achievement of state-level goals (Sharrar, 1992). Now, especially, state-level agencies have been tasked with preparing disaster plans for natural *and* man-made events, including bioterrorism. Local governments, which can be town, city, or county-level, assess and monitor local health problems, develop local leadership and policies, and ensure high-quality services. Many public health clinics act as safety nets for the uninsured and provide a wide range of services including, but not limited to, influenza immunizations, screening programs for hypertension and diabetes, smoking cessation programs, well-baby clinics, substance abuse treatment, and mental health services (LA Health Action, 2007).

Opportunities for Healthcare Management Careers

According to the Association of State and Territorial Health Officers (ASTHO) Council of State Governments (Association of State and Territorial Health Officers [ASTHO], 2004, p. 2), "The most difficult challenge state and local public health agencies face in developing the capacity to respond to terrorist events, emerging infectious diseases, and other public health threats and emergencies is assuring a qualified workforce is available to carry out these functions."

In 2002, ASTHO conducted a survey of state governments and found an aging workforce, increasing retirement rates, high vacancy rates in some states, and high turnover rates. The report cited a lack of qualified applicants, lack of formal education in public health, and reluctance to move to another state as problems in recruitment. In an informal survey of the Maryland Conference of Local Environmental Health Directors (S. Buchbinder, personal communication, September 20, 2007) 5 of the 20 directors indicated they had been unable to fill a food safety position for the past year. Others reported a 75% turnover rate (i.e., three-quarters of the employees had changed in the past year) in food safety positions. Directors reported that most of the turnover occurred because the workers were unprepared for the job, unable to sit for the registered sanitarian exam due to lack of appropriate coursework, or sought upward job mobility. These state-level public health workforce shortages are indicative of the same issues that plague the nation. Not only are people to fill the technical positions in short supply, the managerial positions are turning over due to an aging workforce and baby boomer retirements. As noted in Chapter 1, the job outlook for all healthcare management positions is robust, and public health needs managers as well as biologists, nurses, physicians, epidemiologists, and registered sanitarians.

One excellent way to get your foot into the door of a federal agency is to volunteer or obtain a summer job at the agency where you would like to be employed. The Student Programs page on the HHS website has detailed instructions for applying for these opportunities (HHS, 2008b). In addition, college graduates can apply for internships or the Emerging Leaders Program (ELP; HHS, 2008c), which specifically recruits for administrative positions at entry-level positions. This fast-track program enables the HHS to recruit the brightest and best and encourages applications from people with degrees in business-related areas (HHS, 2008d). Some examples of positions you can obtain with HHS via this fast track include health insurance specialist, budget analyst, and procurement analyst.

Key Managerial Skills and Competencies Required

Managing in a public health agency at any level requires a commitment to serve and protect our citizens, regardless of social standing, educational achievement, or economic circumstances. The poor, elderly, and disadvantaged, especially, are among the populations that public health must serve and protect. You will need a good understanding of the mission, vision, and goals of the agency, as well as an excellent understanding of the populations served and the special needs that may exist. Public health agencies must be responsive to crises. If you choose to work in this area, be aware that the nine-to-five time clock does not apply during a public health emergency; it is a 24/7 responsibility. Strong organizational skills are needed in this environment. The ability to analyze complex and potentially conflicting data and provide recommendations for action based on the data is required. Strong interpersonal skills are a must! This environment is all about teamwork and interagency cooperation. Public health does not exist in a vacuum. Communicable diseases do not respect city, county, state, or national borders. If there is an outbreak of a highly communicable disease, you must be able to work with people across these boundaries to arrive at a plan of action for controlling the epidemic.

Challenges Specific to the Setting

Administrators and managers in public health agencies face many challenges, including, but not limited to staffing, funding issues, the need to obtain grants, the unpredictability of disease, and political changes in election years. In addition, public health agencies are known to have very strict procedures and policies, which are there for many reasons. You must be willing to follow directions and be patient with the layers of bureaucracy that may be required to sign off on your work. In addition, you will probably need a Master of Public Health (MPH) or other graduate degree in a public health-related area in order to advance in your career.

Salary and Compensation

Salaries in public health agencies vary with the level of the agency, geographic region, and the experience the applicant brings to the job. The federal Emerging Leaders Program begins at a GS-9 level, which is approximately $48,000 per year in the Baltimore/Washington, DC, area (U.S. Office of Personnel Management [OPM], 2008). Entry-level state- and county-level administrative positions may require specific skills and technical proficiencies as well as a 4-year degree and experience or a graduate degree. Those positions can range from $35,000 to $45,000 per year, depending on the state and other factors noted above.

Hospitals

General, community, acute care hospitals expanded their roles and became the central focal point of many communities during the latter part of the 20th century. Historically, these facilities served the poor who had no resources, and provided overnight care for individuals who could not be treated on an outpatient basis. More recently, hospitals have expanded to include outpatient services, health education and promotion services, outpatient diagnostic and imaging services, and wellness and fitness services. Hospitals have also secured their positions as the locus of medical technology that has enabled the diagnosis and treatment of a wide variety of medical conditions. In addition, hospitals have developed effective linkages with other organizations to address the needs of their communities.

General, community, acute care hospitals are not the only type of hospital where administrators work. There are specialty hospitals such as children's, rehabilitation, and eye hospitals; long-stay residential hospitals that provide chronic care; teaching hospitals that are part of academic medical centers; and government facilities such as veterans' and military facilities that care for active military personnel and veterans of military service. Hospitals can be categorized in a number of ways, including size, level of care, ownership, and specialty status (Barton, 2007). In 2007, the American Hospital Association (AHA) reported that there were 4,927 community hospitals in the United States. These hospitals have a total of almost 802,000 staffed beds, and had over 37 million admissions. Sixty percent of these facilities were located in urban areas. About one-third of all healthcare expenditures in the United States were hospital expenditures (American Hospital Association [AHA], 2008a).

Opportunities for Healthcare Management Careers

Managers in hospitals work at various levels within the organization, ranging from senior-level administrators to entry-level supervisor positions. These managers oversee the functions that are carried out within the hospitals and include both clinical/patient care functions and nonclinical functions such as public relations, marketing, environmental services, and finance. Examples of senior-level managerial positions in hospitals include administrator or CEO, vice president of finance, chief nursing officer, and vice president of human resources. These senior positions require significant experience and advanced degrees. Examples of entry-level positions held by BS degree holders include director of revenue management, service excellence coordinator, and financial analyst (Thompson, Cockley, & Bopp, 2007).

Currently, about 37% of all healthcare managerial positions are within hospitals. Hospitals will continue to employ the most managers through 2012, although the rate of growth is projected to be slightly below opportunities in other nonhospital settings (BLS, 2007a). Additionally, consolidation among hospitals and expansion of hospital systems as well as efforts to control hospital costs will limit some management opportunities at individual hospitals.

Key Managerial Skills and Competencies Required

Managers in hospitals need strong decision-making and leadership skills. In addition, they should have highly developed interpersonal skills, as they will need to work with staff and colleagues in team structures, as well as provide overall direction for the organization and its units. They need to be able to delegate to their subordinates, seek input, and develop a consensus on actions. Managers in hospitals should possess critical thinking and problem-solving skills, and have the ability to quickly understand issues and identify alternative ways to resolve problems. Hospital managers clearly need strong financial and analytic skills, as well as strategic planning skills, to ensure that their respective units and the overall organization perform well over the long run.

Challenges Specific to the Setting

Although opportunities for management in hospitals continue to be positive, hospital managers face increasing challenges that will impact their managerial effectiveness. These challenges include changes in medical and information technologies and care delivery, continuing competition within the sector, declines in reimbursement, staffing shortages, medical staff relationships, and the accompanying pressures for accountability and transparency (Thompson, 2007). Hospitals are facing higher bad debt loads and pressures from the provision of uncompensated care. In addition, hospitals face increasing demands about disaster preparedness and response, including bioterrorism (Barton, 2007).

Salary and Compensation

Salaries for managers in hospitals will continue to remain favorable. The mean salary for medical and health services managers in general medical and surgical hospitals is $89,590 (BLS, 2007a). Salaries for administrators can range from $35,000 to over $200,000 per year; these latter salaries are given to senior managers with extensive experience who have advanced degrees. Administrators and CEOs can earn over $500,000 per year based on location and size of the hospital, however, these position are limited to those few persons with significant experience and a record of performance (Thompson, 2007). Mean salaries for entry-level administrative personnel in hospitals holding a BS degree can range from $29,000 for the first position to $56,000 in subsequent positions depending upon organizational, market, and personal factors (Thompson et al., 2007). Salaries for mid-level managers can range from $65,000 to $110,000 per year (ACHE, n.d.).

Hospital Systems

Over the past 25 years, more and more hospitals have become part of a hospital system or hospital-based health system. Published data shows that 72% of hospitals operate as part of a system or network (Bazzoli, Chan, Shortell, & D'Aunno, 2000). This trend reflects the fact that hospitals can benefit from affiliations, and research completed on hospital systems has shown that hospitals that provide services through a system are likely to have lower operating costs, superior financial performance, higher efficiency, increased leverage with insurers and managed care organizations, and higher market shares (Bazzoli et al., 2000; Proenca, Rosko, & Dismuke, 2005).

A hospital within a system is defined as a facility that is a part of a corporate body that may own and/or manage health-provider facilities or health-related subsidiaries as well as non-health-related subsidiaries. In other words, the hospitals within a system are under the control of a single organization/company. Hospital systems can operate at different geographic levels including local, regional, and national levels. They also can be nonprofit or for-profit systems. Hospital Corporation of American (HCA) and Tenet Healthcare Corporation are examples of for-profit hospital systems that operate nationally with member hospitals in markets around the country. Catholic Healthcare West, Sisters of Mercy, and Bon Secours Health System are examples of not-for-profit hospital-based health systems that operate in several states.

Opportunities for Healthcare Management Careers

Systems employ managers at both the facility and corporate staff levels. Because hospital-based systems centralize many of their support and administrative functions, many managerial positions are at the corporate or regional offices of these systems. For example, marketing and public relations functions are typically consolidated for the system rather than each facility having an individual marketing director/manager (Thompson, 2009). The same can be said of many central staff functions such as finance, planning, quality management, human resources, information technology and management information services, and legal/regulatory matters. Opportunities for managers and administrative staff in hospital systems will continue to be favorable, as more hospitals join hospital systems or become part of hospital-based health systems. The number of freestanding hospitals (i.e., those that are not part of a system) is expected to continue to decline relative to the number of hospitals in systems.

Key Managerial Skills and Competencies Required

Key skills needed by managers working in hospital systems include strong planning and system-analysis skills, leadership competencies, interpersonal and collaborative skills, and critical reasoning and problem-solving skills. The ability to work across organizations and the ability to forge consensus among staff working at the hospital level are key to success in hospital systems management.

Challenges Specific to the Setting

Key challenges facing managers in hospital systems are providing services across system hospitals using a limited number of central staff, variation in demands across system facilities, and changing system priorities. In addition, the acquisition of more hospitals by a system creates increased workloads for system staff. On the other hand, consolidation among systems may require downsizing of system-level staff.

Salary and Compensation

Salaries can be competitive and are comparable for managers in hospitals. Senior-level and mid-career managers working in a corporate hospital systems office can earn between $65,000 and $110,000 annually (ACHE, n.d.). Mean salaries for entry-level managerial staff with less than 3 years' experience can range from $33,000 to $40,000 per year depending on types of experience and other factors (Thompson et al., 2007). This is consistent with ACHE data that indicate that entry-level managerial personnel in acute care facilities can earn between $40,000 and $60,000 per year (ACHE, n.d.). Entry-level positions within systems for persons having a BS degree include senior financial analyst, marketing coordinator and manager, organizational performance and improvement.

Physician Practices

Physicians invest their lives preparing to go out into the real world to practice medicine. They begin their preparation as premedical students, and must score well on a difficult examination, the Medical College Admission Test (MCAT), to be eligible to apply to medical school. Once in medical school, the majority of physicians in training will take 4 years of advanced work, and along the way must take additional nationally standardized examinations to be considered eligible to graduate and allowed to apply for a residency training program. These postgraduate programs "can be as short as 3 years for family practice or as long as 10 years for cardiothoracic surgery or neurosurgery" (Buchbinder & Buchbinder, 2007, p. 233).

Once they have completed all their education and training, passed their mandatory state licensing examination, which is required to practice medicine, and have become board certified or board eligible (a credential demonstrating competency in a given area) physicians must find the right place to practice what they have been training for during most of their lives. Finding the right practice is very important to physicians, and they have many choices. Two generations ago, it was common for physicians to go into solo practice, that is, they practiced alone, did not have partners, were on call 24/7, and their lives were all medicine, all the time. They had very little leisure or family time.

In 1996, the American Medical Association Council on Medical Services reported that, based on the American Medical Association Socioeconomic Monitoring System data, the proportion of primary care physicians (PCPs) who were self-employed, that is, those physicians who were owners or part owners of a practice or shareholders in their own professional corporation, had fallen dramatically (American Medical Association Council on Medical Services, 1996). All other physicians were considered employed. In 1983, 23% of all practicing PCPs (excluding residents in training) reported being employed; by 1995, that figure had grown to 48%. The proportion of PCPs who were employed increased only 3% between 1983 and 1989, but increased by 22% between 1989 and 1995. Much of the change in physician employment status was due to consolidation of practices and the growth of managed care organizations (MCOs) (Buchbinder, Wilson, Melick, & Powe, 2001).

Coupled with this decline of physician ownership, the percentage of physicians in solo and two-person practices also declined from close to half (40.7%) in 1996, to just under a third (32.5%) in 2004. In 2004, approximately 17.5% of all physicians were in group practices with between six and fifty physicians (Liebhaber & Grossman, 2007). The American Medical Association (AMA) defines group practice as

> The provision of healthcare services by three or more physicians who are formally organized as a legal entity governed by physicians in which business, clinical, and administrative facilities, records, and personnel are shared and the practice goals, objectives, and values are commonly defined. Income from medical services provided by the group are treated as receipts of the group and distributed to some prearranged plan. (Havlicek, 1999, p. 1)

More and more physicians have become employees over time, and more often they are choosing large single- or multi-specialty practices as their employers of choice. Physicians in these settings can have a family, leisure time, better job satisfaction, lower turnover rates, and avoid burnout

(Okie, 2008). The incentives to work in these settings are multifold: better, less-frequent on-call schedule, better benefits, and more vacation time; improved quality of care and customer service, especially in multi-specialty clinics where physicians can send their patients literally next door to see another specialist; and, better reimbursement and increased physician revenues (Buchbinder et al., 2001; Casalino, Devers, Lake, Reed, & Stoddard, 2003; Liebhaber & Grossman, 2007).

Opportunities for Healthcare Management Careers

Physicians are highly trained professionals and are very bright, hardworking people. However, the business of medicine is not part of most medical school curricula and is rarely taught in residency training programs. In order to enable physicians to practice and receive the money they have earned, they need excellent practice managers. Practice managers plan, organize staff, control, direct, and make important decisions. The success of a physician practice is directly related to the quality of its practice manager. With the growth of medium- and large-group physician practices there are increased opportunities for employment in these settings, and well-educated, well-trained practice managers are in short supply. Small medical groups might have one business manager who handles the day-to-day affairs. However, large practices may employ managers at various levels of expertise for different functions and may rely upon their top administrator to manage the strategic direction of the organization (BLS, 2007a). Examples of these other managerial positions include director, health information management and medical records, and billing coordinator.

Key Managerial Skills and Competencies Required

Everything in the medical practice environment—from the cleanliness of the facility, to the profit-and-loss statements, to the magazines and amenities in the patient waiting area—comes under the practice manager's purview. For this setting, you must be a team player, with excellent interpersonal and customer service skills. In addition, business skills such as financial management, marketing, and planning are critical. Strong human resource skills are needed to recruit, select, and retain excellent staff. Compassion and concern for patients coupled with a desire to apply continuous quality improvement techniques in the practice—every day—are musts.

Integrity, honesty, and a strong ethical core are nonnegotiable. Patients entrust you with their medical information, money, and lives. Physicians entrust practice managers with the success of their business and your coworkers trust you to provide them with a positive work environment.

Motivation for lifelong learning and willingness to take continuing education courses to maintain currency and quality of knowledge are critical to success. This is a fluid, dynamic area of healthcare management. The knowledge base changes daily. You must be willing to keep up with the needs of the practice and be able to navigate the "whitewater rapids" of the physician practice environment. The Medical Group Management Association (MGMA) is the premier association for becoming a practice manager. The MGMA has online tools to help you decide whether practice management is for you, as well as an extensive outline of the body of knowledge needed for practice management (Medical Group Management Association [MGMA], 2008a, 2008b). A practice manager can earn board certification and become a Certified Medical Practice Executive (CMPE), and over time earn Fellowship through the American College of Medical Practice Executives (ACMPE). Much like board certification for physicians, and Fellowship in the American College of Healthcare Executives (ACHE) for hospital managers, these examinations are voluntary demonstrations of knowledge, skills, and abilities as a practice manager and act as proxies for the quality of the services provided (MGMA, 2008b).

Challenges Specific to the Setting

Although there is economy of scale and better negotiation with insurance companies for payment for services in large medical group practices, reimbursement remains the number one challenge for physician practice management (Casalino et al., 2003). Health insurance plans change almost daily, it seems, and it is not uncommon for a practice to have one administrator whose main responsibility is to update health insurance benefits information. Some plans require a referral, others require co-pays, and some cover one procedure, but not another, similar, procedure. It is the responsibility of the practice manager to monitor and control the revenue cycle from start to finish. Health insurance claims are denied daily. The challenge is to find the root cause for the denial and resubmit the claim in a timely fashion to ensure maximum revenues for the organization (Milburn, 2007). Competition among physician practices is another significant challenge, as well as competition with other ambulatory care centers and programs. As a result, physician practices have formalized marketing and communication programs to foster greater consumer preference.

Salary and Compensation

Salaries and compensation in physician practice settings will vary by the size of the practice, the number of physicians, the level of responsibility, and your experience. In 2006, according to the BLS, the median annual earnings for administrators in physicians' offices were $67,540 (BLS, 2007a). Keep in mind this figure does not represent an entry-level salary, but the range of salaries in these settings with this number at the middle of the range.

Assisted Living Facilities

Assisted living facilities (ALFs) emerged in a formal way in the early 1990s as a necessary alternative to address the housing and care needs of an aging population. For many years, group and boarding homes provided supervised care and assistance to older adults. As Americans are living longer and experiencing more chronic diseases that require daily assistance, individuals are in need of residential care options to help them. In addition, growth in the older-age cohorts due to the aging of the baby boom generation, and their increasing health needs, has led to increased demand for ALF services Thompson, 2007). ALFs provide a range of services, including assistance with activities of daily living, medication management, housekeeping and laundry services, social and recreation activities, health promotion and exercise programs, transportation, and meals, in addition to housing accommodations (Assisted Living Federation of America [ALFA], 2008; Pratt, 1999). The goal of assisted living is to enhance the capabilities of older adults to live as independently as possible. Administrators and other managerial personnel must devote time and attention to the residents and their families to enable the residents to reach this goal.

Assisted living has witnessed explosive growth in the past 20 years. In the 1980s and 1990s, many for-profit companies entered the ALF business. Several of these companies are publicly traded, which means that they issue stock to purchasing shareholders. According to the Assisted Living Federation of America (ALFA), the largest ALF firm in 2008 was Sunrise Senior Living, which had a resident capacity in excess of 32,500 in 458 properties around the United States. Other firms providing ALF services include Emeritus Senior Living, Brookdale Senior Living, Sunwest Management, and HCR ManorCare (ALFA, 2008).

Opportunities for Healthcare Management Careers

Because of the demand for ALF services and the rapid growth of these facilities, there are many opportunities for administrators and other managerial personnel. Positions include administrator, director of activities, director of admissions and marketing, and director of community relations. Candidates for these positions will require a minimum of a bachelor's degree; many successful administrators and department managers for ALFs have only a BS degree. Historically, ALF administrators have not been required to be licensed as administrators, but the landscape is quickly changing in this regard. Several states are either now requiring licensure or are considering licensure for ALF administrators. For example, Arizona, Idaho, Nevada, New Jersey, and South Carolina currently require ALF administrators to be licensed (LongTermCareEducation.com, 2008).

Key Managerial Skills and Competencies Required

Managerial skills needed in this setting include a passion for serving the elderly and a caring orientation toward meeting the needs of the elderly. Strong organizational, interpersonal, and collaborative skills are necessary because administrators typically have close working relationships with staff, residents, and residents' families due to the small size of these facilities. Financial management skills are also essential.

Challenges Specific to the Setting

Administrators and managerial personnel at ALFs face several challenges. These include keeping costs under control to remain competitive, staffing turnover and shortages, and increased competition by other sectors of the long-term care industry such as nursing homes, retirement communities, and rehabilitation centers.

Salary and Compensation

The number of positions in ALFs is expected to increase in the next 15–20 years given the growth in the older-age cohorts. An increase in the number of firms specializing in ALFs is likely given the attractiveness of private payment for services. Many of the new firms entering the market may focus on specialized services, such as dementia care, as well as a focus on specific geographic or local markets. Opportunities in lead administrator jobs as well as director roles are likely. Annual salaries for managerial personnel in ALFs are competitive and may range from $40,000 to $55,000 for an entry-level administrator and $65,000 to $85,000 for a mid-career ALF administrator (Long Term Care Education.com, 2008).

Nursing Homes

Today's older adults move in and out of nursing homes after a hospitalization or accident. Family and friends provide the majority of long-term care services needed by older adults. Currently less than 5% of the older population is in a nursing home and, for a growing number of older adults, the facility is a short-term rehabilitation-and-recovery stop (D. Wagner, personal communication, November 25, 2008). Nursing homes are best thought of as one stop along a continuum in long-term care, the goal of which is "to be able to access the configuration of services needed by an individual according to his or her unique needs, and to modify the set of services provided as a person's needs change" (Evashwick & Riedel, 2004, p. 18). Extended care facilities can include skilled nursing facilities, step-down unit/transitional care unit, and subacute units.

In 2002, nursing homes provided services to 2.5 million clients per year (Evashwick & Riedel, 2004, p. 31). Services provided to residents in these facilities include, but are not limited to:

- "Physical therapy
- Occupational therapy
- Speech therapy
- Respiratory therapy
- Alzheimer's disease and dementia treatment
- Cancer and hematologic therapy
- Cardiovascular disease treatment/therapy
- Neurological and neuromuscular diseases treatment/therapy
- Orthopedic rehabilitation
- Pain therapy

- Pulmonary disease treatment/therapy
- Para/quadriplegic impairments treatment/therapy
- Stroke and trauma recovery treatment/therapy
- Wound care
- Renal dialysis
- HIV/AIDS treatment/therapy
- Mental health and substance abuse treatment/therapy"

Some nursing homes specialize in specific areas for which they have expertise, such as HIV/AIDS care or Alzheimer's disease and other dementias. All nursing homes assist residents, as needed, with their activities of daily living (ADLs), such as eating, bathing, toileting, grooming, walking, and dressing (Evashwick & Riedel, 2004, p. 33).

Opportunities for Healthcare Management Careers

The aging of the baby boomers means a plethora of opportunities for services to this population. As this large generation heads into retirement, they bring their personalities with them along with their knowledge of how systems work, their work ethic, and demands for a good quality of life. They will not want to be in a skilled nursing facility (SNF) or nursing home, unless it is the absolute last resort. That means they will be sicker, need more intensive care, and better caregiving as the SNF becomes nearly indistinguishable from an acute care hospital. Employment opportunities in nursing and personal care facilities are projected to increase 22% between 2000 and 2010 (BLS, 2007a). Job opportunities for managers in these settings will range from director of admissions, to billing manager and nursing home administrator. Opportunities for entry-level positions for those with a bachelor's degree are excellent, and as with all other healthcare settings, the more education you obtain, the better your opportunities for advancement.

Key Managerial Skills and Competencies Required

The licensed nursing home administrator (NHA) is responsible for management of the SNF and plays a key role in the quality of care and the quality of life of the people he or she serves (Dana & Olson, 2007). However, every employee in a nursing home is responsible for providing safe, compassionate, and dignified care to the residents. To work in these settings, you must be respectful of the residents and passionate about ensuring good quality of care. You must have excellent teamwork skills, be organized, and resourceful. Nursing homes, like hospitals, are 24/7 facilities. Hours can be long, and if there is a crisis or a resident in need, it may be up to you to stay at the resident's side to ensure he or she receives the appropriate care. The abilities to multitask and work with people from diverse cultures are critical. Due to direct-care staffing shortages, many nursing homes employ Certified Nurse Aides or Nursing Assistants (CNAs) from other cultures, sometimes from other nations. Conflict resolution, cultural sensitivity, and the ability to remain calm under stress are some of the emotional intelligences you will need in these settings. Above all, you must remember: It is *always* about the resident!

Challenges Specific to the Setting

One key challenge in nursing home is staff turnover. **Turnover**, also called job exit or quit, can be involuntary or voluntary. Involuntary turnover occurs when someone is terminated or fired. Voluntary turnover occurs when the employee says, "I quit!" Turnover is usually expressed as a proportion, so for example, if you have 100 employees and 10 quit in a year, the turnover rate is 10%. Sometimes turnover can be fortuitous, especially if the person who leaves has been a problem employee. However, when voluntary turnover rates are high, the phenomenon indicates underlying issues which are often due to poor management. Turnover rates in nursing homes are higher than any other setting in health care (Stone, 2000). Some troubled nursing homes have turnover rates among CNAs of 100% (W. Nelson, personal communication, February 20, 2008). That means that *every* CNA in that nursing home has quit that year. It is a challenge to recruit, select, and retain good CNAs. As a manager, you must remember CNAs provide the majority of the direct, hands-on care to vulnerable residents. It is critical to conduct criminal background checks to ensure you do not hire elder abusers, predators, or thieves. However, you also want to recognize and reward those who are high performers and who are good caregivers, otherwise they may become overwhelmed and leave for other positions.

Another key challenge in nursing homes is regulation. Due to abuses in the past, nursing homes, in some states, are subject to more regulations than hospitals. In certain states, the state regulations are more stringent than federal regulations. Nursing homes must meet quality standards or they risk losing Medicare and Medicaid reimbursements. Long-term care insurance is a luxury for most elderly individuals. Medicare provides 100% of expenses for the first 20 days of skilled nursing care after 3 consecutive days of hospitalization, not including the day of discharge. This nursing care must be physician-prescribed to be covered by Medicare. For days 21–100 in a skilled nursing facility, the beneficiary must pay a significant co-payment. Beginning with day 101, the resident is responsible for all costs (Centers for Medicare and Medicaid Services [CMS], 2008a). Medicaid will begin only after a resident has spent down to poverty and becomes eligible to receive these funds. Balancing access, cost of care, and quality of care is the tightrope you will walk in this setting.

Salary and Compensation

Salaries and compensation in nursing homes will vary by the size, number of residents, whether the home is part of a large corporation, the level of responsibility, and your experience. In 2006, according to the BLS, the median annual earnings for nursing care facilities were $66,730 (BLS, 2007a). Keep in mind this figure does not represent an entry-level salary, but the range of salaries in these settings, for a variety of jobs including nursing home administrator, with this number at the middle of the range.

Retirement Communities

As noted earlier, our population is aging and people have become savvy, discerning customers of healthcare services. Along the continuum of long-term care, we have already described assisted living facilities and nursing homes. Think of a continuing care retirement community (CCRC) as another stop along this continuum. CCRCs have it all: housing, social services, and health care. If you visit a CCRC, you will find a fitness center, a convenience store, transportation to shopping and entertainment, an elegant dining room and a casual cafe, as well as independent living, assisted living, and nursing homes. This is the most expensive of all long-term care options; very few people can afford this "country club" lifestyle. There is an entry fee to become a member that can range from five to six figures, and may not be refundable. Monthly maintenance fees "usually range from $650 to $3,500, and may be increased from year to year due to inflation" (CMS, 2008b). Some CCRCs are not all inclusive and may charge additional fees for long-term care costs. Little at-home care is provided; if a resident wants a companion or helper, it is an out-of-pocket cost. And, finally, to be eligible to enter the CCRC, the applicant must be in good health (CMS, 2008b).

Opportunities for Healthcare Management Careers

As noted before, the aging of the baby boomers means a plethora of opportunities for services to this population. As this large generation heads into retirement, these people bring their personalities with them, along with their knowledge of how systems work, their work ethic, and with CCRCs, especially, demands for a good quality of life. Employment opportunities in nursing and personal care facilities are projected to increase 22% between 2000 and 2010 (BLS, 2007a). Job titles in CCRCs can include director of admissions, director of dining room services, billing manager, and nursing home administrator. Opportunities for entry-level positions for those with a bachelor's degree are excellent, and as with all other healthcare settings, the more education you obtain, the better your opportunities for advancement.

Key Managerial Skills and Competencies Required

As noted above, the residents in CCRCs are affluent and, for the most part, able to pay and expect to receive quality services. Customer service and excellent teamwork skills are critical. CCRCs require a blend of hotel and hospitality management skills and compassion for the elderly. One day a very demanding resident can be well and able to take care of himself or herself, and the next day, he or she may experience an event that requires a move to the nursing home portion of the CCRC. This is traumatic for the resident; his or her ability for self-care may have been compromised. You must have the emotional intelligence and empathy to work with these residents and treat everyone with dignity. As with nursing homes, every employee in a CCRC is responsible for providing compassionate, safe, dignified care to the residents. To work in these settings, you must be respectful of the residents and passionate about ensuring good quality of care. Above all, you must remember: It is *always* about the resident!

Challenges Specific to the Setting

CCRCs are subject to the same regulations as nursing homes, and are accredited by the Commission on Accreditation of Rehabilitation Facilities (Commission on Accreditation of Rehabilitation Facilities [CARF], 2008). In addition, they fall under the auspices of state and federal regulations for the nursing home portion of the facility, with the same challenges previously noted under nursing homes. Employee turnover is less of an issue in CCRCs due to the fact that they are able to pay higher salaries to employees. The same due diligence applies in recruiting, selecting, and retaining employees as in nursing homes, however, ensuring excellent customer service skills in staff is a daily challenge for managers in CCRCs.

Salary and Compensation

As with nursing homes, salaries and compensation in CCRCs will vary by the size, number of residents, whether it is part of a large corporation, the level of responsibility, and your experience. In 2006, according to the BLS, the median annual earnings for nursing care facilities were $66,730 (BLS, 2007a). Again, keep in mind this figure does not represent an entry-level salary, but the range of salaries in these settings for a variety of jobs including nursing home administrator, with this number at the middle of the range.

Wellness/Fitness Centers

Another area of recent growth in health services is the area of wellness and fitness centers and services. Over the past 30 years, consumers, employers, and healthcare professionals have recognized the value of exercise and fitness in maintaining good health. Hospitals and physicians first saw the need for wellness and fitness programs as an outgrowth of the medical treatment provided in hospitals, for example, cardiac rehabilitation programs (Seymour, 2003). In the late 1970s and early 1980s, hospitals began acquiring fitness centers to create subsidiaries focused on health but also to emphasize those services viewed as revenue generators and feeders to other hospital-based services. Private entrepreneurs adopted the concept and developed their own fitness centers, wellness programs, and clubs in order to meet a growing need for personal wellness and fitness.

There are two basic models for the operation of wellness and fitness centers: health organization-sponsored wellness/fitness centers, and private clubs and centers. The first group may include wellness centers that are part of an existing healthcare organization, such as a hospital, retirement community, and/or physician practice. Each of these models issues memberships (retirement communities also serve existing residents) and provides a range of services for members, including access to fitness equipment, health education and promotion classes, exercise and fitness classes, and personalized instruction and coaching. Significant growth has occurred in the number of private health clubs. A recent initiative in wellness is business-sponsored wellness and fitness centers, where the company has its own fitness facility to serve its employees and their dependents.

Opportunities for Healthcare Management Careers

Management opportunities in the wellness and fitness area include directors of these programs as well as directors of certain functions, such as membership and marketing, health promotion and education, and finance. Because of the importance and emphasis on health promotion and fitness, the expected growth in these management jobs is excellent, although management-prepared persons may be competing with health education and fitness specialists.

Key Managerial Skills and Competencies Required

Skills needed by managers within wellness and fitness organizations include high customer service and interpersonal skills, strong financial skills, well-developed marketing skills, and competencies in competitive analysis and strategy development.

Challenges Specific to the Setting

Specific challenges to managers in this setting include intense competition among fitness facilities, retention of members, and relationship building with established healthcare organizations.

Salary and Compensation

Salaries for fitness center directors can range from $50,000 to $105,000 per year, according to Salary.com (2008). This range reflects market type, member volume, size of center, and scope of services provided.

NON-DIRECT CARE SETTINGS

Associations

Associations are groups of people and professionals who join together under an organizational umbrella because they have common goals and concerns. According to ASAE and the Center for Excellence in Association Leadership (2008a), there are 1.8 million associations in the United States. Although not all of these are not-for-profit or related to health care, associations employ thousands of people. Professional and trade associations exist for many reasons. ASAE and the Center for Excellence in Association Leadership (2008a) offers the following list of the most common goals and benefits associations provide to members:

- "Education/professional development
- Information, research, and statistics
- Standards, codes of ethics, and certification
- Forum (face-to-face or virtual) to discuss common problems and solutions
- Service/mission-oriented volunteerism and community service
- Provide a community, network, "home," identity, and participation"

Two of the leading associations in public health and medicine, the American Public Health Association (APHA) and the American Medical Association (AMA), have been in existence since the 1800s. The APHA has been in existence since 1872, and is the "largest and most diverse organization of public health professionals in the world" (American Public Health Association [APHA], 2008). The AMA was created in 1847, because of concerns about the appalling lack of quality in medical school graduates at that time. The Council on Medical Education was formed as part of the AMA, and Abraham Flexner presented his report on medical education in the United States and Canada that included recommendations on closing substandard schools (American Medical Association [AMA], 2008). The American Hospital Association was established in 1898 and now represents over 5,000 hospitals and 37,000 individual members (AHA, 2008b). The Association of University Programs in

Health Administration "grew out of the efforts of the W.K. Kellogg Foundation to professionalize the management of hospitals following World War II" (AUPHA, 2008). AUPHA now represents over 140 undergraduate and graduate healthcare management programs in North America. As health care grows, associations that represent healthcare organizations and professionals will grow, too. There are national associations focused on specific health facilities or issues, such as the Association of Children's Hospitals and the American Urological Association. In addition to national associations described above, there are many state and local level associations that address member needs of various healthcare providers, such as physicians.

Opportunities for Healthcare Management Careers

According to the BLS, "advocacy, grant making, and civic organizations had 1.2 million wage and salary jobs in 2006, with 74% in civic, social, professional, and similar organizations." It is anticipated that jobs will increase in this area by about 13% between 2006 and 2016 (BLS, 2008).

Key Managerial Skills and Competencies Required

Associations need all of the traditional management skills-planning, organizing staffing, controlling, directing, and decision making—in addition to functional areas like finance, accounting, marketing, advertising, technology, communications, public relations, government relations, legal, membership marketing, grant-writing, and conference and event planning (ASAE and the Center for Excellence in Association Leadership, 2008a). One of the most important areas in any association is membership marketing. Members are the lifeblood of an association. Retention of current members is just as important, if not more than, recruitment of new members. It is everyone's job to provide excellent customer service.

Challenges Specific to the Setting

Since associations advocate for their members, in this environment it is your job to stay one step ahead of your membership. This is not an easy task, and it sometimes requires exquisite political finesse to convince your members that the next big trend in the field is something that is potentially contrary to how they've been doing business. The politics of association management is not something you learn overnight. It is a skill that takes years of observation and paying your dues in the trenches, working late at night to make sure every event is a success. Good association managers look for mentors in the field and take advantage of continuing education opportunities. The premier organization for these educational opportunities is the ASAE and the Center for Excellence in Association Leadership (2008a). Becoming a Certified Association Executive (CAE) is one way to demonstrate competency in this professional arena. The CAE examination covers a wide range of management skills, as well as association-specific domains (ASAE and the Center for Excellence in Association Leadership, 2008b).

Salary and Compensation

Salaries and compensation in associations will vary by the size of the organization, the number of members, the level of responsibility, and your experience. Most associations are small; according to the BLS (2008) "about 9 out of 10 advocacy, grant-making, and civic organizations employ 20 or fewer employees." The BLS reports a wide range of annual salaries by position, from director of volunteers at $41,000 to executive director at $149,000 (BLS, 2008). Competition for the top jobs in associations is intense, so be aware that if you want to become the CEO of an association, you may have to start at a smaller association with less income and pay your dues in time and continuing education in order to be able to move to larger associations with higher paid positions.

Consulting Firms

As healthcare organizations have become increasingly complex and highly regulated, their need for consultants has increased. Consulting firms have experienced significant growth in the past 20 years as healthcare organizations have realized the need for outside assistance based on a lack of in-house expertise, time, and/or staff. Consulting firms provide strategic, operational, and financial assistance (Thompson, 2007). They offer technical expertise in assisting healthcare organizations and government health organizations in a variety of activities such as recruitment, staffing and human resources issues, evaluation of new services, process improvement and reengineering, cost management systems, and information technology. For a health services organization, the benefits of using a consultant are: 1) expertise that the organization doesn't have; 2) quick assistance to the firm; and 3) an objective viewpoint.

Opportunities for Healthcare Management Careers

Consulting firms range from small local firms employing just a few professional staff, to large national and multinational companies with offices across the United States, and in some cases, throughout the world. Examples of the latter are Booz Allen Hamilton, Ernst and Young, and BearingPoint. There are general management consulting firms that provide assistance to healthcare organizations and there are healthcare management consulting firms that specialize in issues specific to healthcare organizations. In addition, there are specialist consulting firms that focus on specific functional areas of concern to healthcare organizations including human resources recruitment, staffing, training, and development; financial analysis and revenue management; marketing and business development; and patient safety and quality improvement, for example. Also, some consulting firms are part of healthcare product organizations, such as manufacturers of information technology and medical devices.

Medium to large firms carry out their activities on a team basis, where partners or senior consultants direct project teams comprised of consultants, research associates, and research assistants. A consultant or research associate may work on different teams addressing projects for different clients at the same time. Senior consultants must be able to handle several projects simultaneously and be willing to continue to market the firm in order to have a steady stream of business.

Opportunities to work in consulting are expected to be very good during the next 10–25 years (Thompson, 2007). As direct care organizations deal with staffing issues and reimbursement constraints that affect workforce availability, organizations will tend to rely on consultants to get their work done. However, use of consultants may decline at times when healthcare organizations face budget challenges.

Key Managerial Skills and Competencies Required

Key skills of consultants include strong conceptual skills to help identify consulting needs of organizations, and strong technical and interpersonal skills to work with team members as well as staff from client organizations. Consultants need to have strong organizational skills, and be highly motivated and goal oriented so that multiple tasks can be successfully completed.

Challenges Specific to the Setting

Challenges facing consultants include the fast pace of the work, effectively multitasking by simultaneously addressing several clients and projects, staying current with knowledge of best practices, innovation, and trends in the healthcare system, and being flexible and available when the client organization needs assistance. Competition among consulting firms for client business can be a significant negative force on an individual firm.

Salary and Compensation

Salaries can be quite high in consulting, as the work is fast paced, demanding, and frequently travel intensive. Consulting firms have developed employee-friendly work environments where flexible work locations (e.g., home via telecommuting), flextime, and compressed work weeks may be available. However, consultants' work will depend on the necessary efforts to get the job done and may require long hours. Many firms have an incentive compensation system in place where, on top of a base salary, employees can earn additional compensation according to the firm's overall business volume or as a portion of the total business generated by the consultant. Base yearly salaries for consultants can range from $73,300 to $118,600 for an information services consultant, and $63,990 to $108,600 for an organizational development consultant (Salary.com, 2008). An executive recruiter working for a staff recruitment firm may earn between $50,680 and $100,680 per year (Salary.com, 2008). Senior consultants and partners in consulting firms can earn significantly higher annual salaries.

Medical Suppliers

Direct care organizations rely on many materials and supplies to provide care to their patients. In addition, they rely on medical and information technologies to remain efficient, effective, and state of the art. Innovation in and development of medical technology has resulted in health services organizations adopting more and more technology. Direct care settings want to be able to provide the latest and highest quality diagnostic and treatment technology to remain competitive. Medical equipment firms produce and distribute highly specialized equipment that includes computed tomography (CT) scanners; magnetic resonance imaging (MRI) scanners; surgical equipment, such as robots; cardiovascular devices, such as implantable defibrillators and pacemakers; radiation therapy equipment for treating cancer; and orthopedic implantable devices for hips and knees. Medical equipment adds value to the services that hospitals and other healthcare providers offer to their patients (Burns, 2002). In addition to medical equipment firms, there are many firms that produce and distribute basic and specialized medical supplies to healthcare organizations.

Opportunities for Healthcare Management Careers

Hospitals and other direct care provider organizations, such as physician practices and ambulatory clinics, represent a significant market for medical equipment and supplies. Healthcare managers work as research, sales, marketing, and analytical staff for the research, development, and marketing of this equipment. Companies that produce this technology can be either large, multinational firms or national firms. For example, Siemens and General Electric (GE) manufacture and distribute scanners and other diagnostic information technology. Medtronics and Synthes manufacture cardiovascular technologies and implantable orthopedic devices, respectively. Cardinal Health is one of the leading medical product suppliers for hospitals in the United States. Examples of managerial positions in these types of firms include sales representative, director of sales, vice president of sales and marketing, product line manager, and district sales manager.

Key Managerial Skills and Competencies Required

These managers may direct staff within the company, or if in marketing and sales, work with customers who will purchase their products. Therefore, they may interact with and sell to clinicians, and finance and purchasing staff at hospitals, physician practices, clinics, and surgical centers. Managers in medical equipment firms must be self-directed, motivated, organized, and able to multitask. They must have strong organizational skills, be excellent communicators, and have highly developed interpersonal skills.

Challenges Specific to the Setting

The challenges managers face in this setting include intense competition among firms, extensive regulation of company products, and uncertainty regarding reimbursement from insurers for newly developed medical technologies.

Salary and Compensation

Due to competitive pressures and the importance of quality care and the dependence of direct care organizations on technology, materials, and supplies, medical equipment research, sales, and marketing is promising as a career. Entry-level annual salaries for general sales representatives can range from $38,000 to $71,000, while sales director salaries can range from $101,000 to over $200,000 per year (Salary.com, 2008).

Managed Care Organizations/Health Insurers

The commercial health insurance business has grown significantly since 1990. This is due primarily to the large number of persons who receive health coverage through their place of employment. America's Health Insurance Plans reports that over 201 million individuals are covered by private health insurance; 96% of large employers and 43% of small employers offer health insurance (America's Health Insurance Plans [AHIP], n.d.). Over 469,000 people work directly in health insurance and over 880,000 work in other health insurance-related jobs (AHIP, n.d.).

The health insurance business has consolidated over the past 10 years, as a few large firms have acquired smaller firms. The top firms in 2007 in terms of member enrollment were Wellpoint (30.2 million), United Health Group (17 million), Aetna (13.9 million), Health Care Services Corporation (12.1 million), Humana (11.4 million), CIGNA Healthcare (9 million), and Kaiser Permanente (8.8 million) (Managed Care Digest, n.d.). These firms have adopted managed care principles and plans in order to help employers control costs, and currently offer a range of plans (e.g., health maintenance organizations [HMOs], preferred provider organizations [PPOs], and other networks) to employers and their employees in many markets around the country. These companies, now commonly known as managed care organizations (MCOs), offer products specifically targeting the Medicare and Medicaid populations, and also operate HMO, network, and case management plans providing services to the enrollees in many states.

Opportunities for Healthcare Management Careers

MCOs carry out a range of functions that address recruitment, support, and customer service for members; network development; contracting and support of participating physicians, hospitals, and other direct care providers; actuarial and underwriting, billing, and reimbursement functions; sales and marketing functions targeting employers for the group market and individuals for the individual market; public relations; and corporate responsibility functions. These firms have a variety of managerial positions and administrative support positions that are needed for the MCO to complete its business. Examples of positions include vice president of sales and marketing, vice president of finance, director of provider relations, network development specialist, director of marketing, reimbursement analyst and member services coordinator, contracting specialist, and director of quality improvement.

Key Managerial Skills and Competencies Required

Skills needed by managers in the MCO setting include critical thinking; strong analytic and problem-solving abilities; financial comprehension and computational skills; marketing savvy and strong interpersonal skills, particularly for those who work in member services and network development/provider relations.

Challenges Specific to the Setting

Some challenges facing managers in MCOs include uncertainty regarding the future of a national health insurance plan for the United States, continuing consolidation of the industry, and variation in the number of employers who are offering health insurance to their employees.

Salary and Compensation

The growth opportunities in the MCO sector for managers and administrative support personnel are forecast to be very good given the importance of health insurance and the desire of employers to control costs (Thompson, 2007). Salaries are competitive and will vary by type, size, and location of firm, among other factors. ACHE reports that salaries for entry-level administrative staff in MCOs can range from $40,000 to $60,000, mid-level management from $55,000 to $85,000, and senior management from $150,000 to over $250,000 per year (ACHE, n.d.).

Pharmaceutical Firms

Thanks to pharmaceutical firms' research and development, chronic diseases that once killed people can now be treated with new drugs, enabling citizens to live longer, productive lives. According to PhRMA (2008), "companies spent an estimated $44.5 billion to discover and develop new medicines in 2007." Additionally, it can take 10 to 15 years to bring a new medicine to market. To compound matters, once the 20-year patent life for a drug expires, generic drugs can be manufactured and compete with the brand-name medication. This enormous, long-term investment requires a large, well-educated, competitive sales force to bring revenues in to balance the books, recoup the past costs of doing business, and not go bankrupt. Pharmaceutical firms are looking for graduates of healthcare management programs with solid business skills and an understanding of how health care really works.

Opportunities for Healthcare Management Careers

In 2006, pharmaceutical and medicine manufacturing provided almost one-third of a million jobs in the United States. Of this, about 3% or about 9,000 jobs were in sales. According to the BLS (2007b), the job outlook in pharmaceutical firms is excellent and wage and salary jobs are expected to increase by 24% over the 2006–2016 period.

Key Managerial Skills and Competencies Required

In this extremely competitive field, those who have previous sales experience are preferred. The companies want to know if you have the competitive edge needed to close a deal, because past behavior predicts future behavior. A bachelor's degree is required in this field and a good ability to understand the science behind the development of the drugs is a must. Continuing education is part of the job. The companies invest extensively in ongoing education and training programs; you must achieve a certain grade on the examinations in order to land the job and to progress once you have secured the position. Pharmaceutical sales representatives must be self-directed, motivated, organized, and able to multitask. In addition, strong organizational, communication, and interpersonal skills are required.

Challenges Specific to the Setting

Coupled with burgeoning scientific discoveries and breakthroughs, there are concerns about the rising costs of health care, in general, and pharmaceuticals in specific. The Kaiser Family Foundation reported that prescription drug spending has increased "sharply in recent years, growing at 12% annually between 1990 and 2000" (Kaiser Family Foundation [KFF], 2008). Politically, the pharmaceutical industry is in the spotlight, and major drug companies are working hard to demonstrate how they contribute to the economy and the health of the nation. On a day-to-day basis, this means that you, as a pharmaceutical sales representative, may be the recipient of questions about your industry. You will need to be informed about what your firm is doing to give back to the community and to help people who cannot afford expensive prescriptions. In addition to fielding some uncomfortable political questions, your day-to-day schedule may be filled with rejections: "The doctor is out," "The doctor is too busy to see you," "The doctor doesn't have time to see drug reps," and so on. Competition between drug companies is fierce, and the doctor's office may have just seen your competitor that same day. You must be prepared to be turned away, and you must be resilient and persistent—all with a smile and a polite response.

Salary and Compensation

If you are willing to work hard, put in long hours, maintain your educational edge, and are competitive, you can do very well in pharmaceutical sales. Median base salaries plus bonuses can range between $46,000 and $86,000, and six-figure incomes can top the charts for this position (Salary.com, 2008). Along with the salary, bonuses, and a benefits package with healthcare insurance, many pharmaceutical firms also provide their sales representatives with a car or a car allowance.

REFERENCES

Accreditation Association for Ambulatory Health Care. (2008). *What is the accreditation association?* Retrieved November 25, 2008, from http://www.aaahc.org/eweb/dynamicpage.aspx?webcode=home

American College of Healthcare Executives. (n.d.) Retrieved October 18, 2008, from http://www.ache.org/CARSVCS/CareerOverviews/managedcare_entry.cfm and http://www.ache.org/CARSVCS/CareerOverviews/acutecare_entry.cfm

American Hospital Association. (2008a, August). *The cost of caring: Sources of growth in spending for hospital care.* Retrieved November 6, 2008, from http://www.aha.org/aha/issues/Affordability/resources.html

American Hospital Association. (2008b). *About the American hospital association.* Retrieved November 27, 2008, from http://www.aha.org/aha/about/index.html

American Medical Association. (2008). *Illustrated highlights of AMA history.* Retrieved November 26, 2008, from http://www.ama-assn.org/ama/pub/category/1915.html

American Medical Association Council on Medical Services. (1996). *Trends in physician practice consolidation. CMS report 9-1-96.* Chicago: American Medical Association.

American Public Health Association. (2008). *About us.* Retrieved November 26, 2008, from http://www.apha.org/about/

America's Health Insurance Plans. (n.d.) Retrieved October 18, 2008, from http://www.ahipresearch.org/PDFs/StateData/StateDataUS.pdf

ASAE and the Center for Excellence in Association Leadership. (2008a). *Association FAQ.* Retrieved November 26, 2008, from http://www.asaecenter.org/AdvocacyOutreach/contentASAEOnly.cfm?ItemNumber=16341&navItemNumber=14992

ASAE and the Center for Excellence in Association Leadership. (2008b). *Certified association executive program.* Retrieved November 27, 2008, from http://www.asaecenter.org/YourCareer/contentcae.cfm?ItemNumber=16097&navItemNumber=14985

Assisted Living Federation of America. (2008, April) Largest assisted living providers. *Assisted Living Executive.* Retrieved November 6, 2008, from http://www.alfa.org

Association of State and Territorial Health Officers Council of State Governments. (2004). *State public health employee worker shortage report.* Retrieved November 20, 2008, from http://www.sph.umn.edu/img/assets/15702/WorkforceShortageReportFinal.pdf

Association of University Programs in Health Administration. (2008). *About AUPHA: History.* Retrieved November 27, 2008, from http://www.aupha.org/i4a/pages/index.cfm?pageid=3287

Baer, J. (1996). *Send this jerk the bedbug letter.* Berkeley, CA: Ten Speed Press.

Barr, K. W., & Breindel, C. L. (2004). Ambulatory care. In L. F. Wolper (Ed.), *Healthcare administration: Planning, implementing, and managing organized delivery systems* (pp. 507–546). Sudbury, MA: Jones and Bartlett.

Barton, P. L. (2007). *Understanding the U.S. health services system* (3rd ed.). Chicago: HAP/AUPHA Press.

Bazzoli, G. J., Chan, B., Shortell, S. M., & D'Aunno, T. (2000). The financial performance of hospitals belonging to health networks and systems. *Inquiry, 37,* 234–252.

Buchbinder, S. B., & Buchbinder, D. (2007). Managing healthcare professionals. In S. B. Buchbinder & N. H. Shanks (Eds.), *Introduction to healthcare management* (p. 233). Sudbury, MA: Jones and Bartlett.

Buchbinder, S. B., Wilson, M. H., Melick, C. F., & Powe, N. R. (2001). Primary care physician job satisfaction and turnover. *American Journal of Managed Care, 7,* 701–713. Retrieved November 25, 2008, from http://www.ajmc.com/files/articlefiles/AJMC2001julBUCHBINDER701.pdf

Burns, L. R. (2002). *The healthcare value chain: Producers, purchasers and providers.* San Francisco: Jossey-Bass.

Casalino, L. P., Devers, K. J., Lake, T. K., Reed, M., & Stoddard, J. J. (2003). Benefits of and barriers to large medical group practice in the United States. *Arch Intern Med, 163,* 1958–1964.

Center for Medicare and Medicaid Services. (2008a). *Medicare coverage of skilled nursing facility care.* Retrieved November 25, 2008, from http://www.medicare.gov/Publications/Pubs/pdf/10153.pdf

Center for Medicare and Medicaid Services. (2008b). *Paying for long-term care: Continuing care retirement communities.* Retrieved November 26, 2008, from http://www.medicare.gov/LongTermCare/Static/ContinuingCare.asp?dest=NAV%7CPaying%7CHomeEquity%7CContinuingCare#TabTop

Commission on Accreditation of Rehabilitation Facilities. (2008). *About CARF.* Retrieved November 26, 2008, from http://www.carf.org/

Dana, B., & Olson, D. (2007). *Effective leadership in long-term care: The need and the opportunity.* American College of Health Care Administrators Position Paper. Retrieved November 25, 2008, from http://www.achca.org/content/pdf/ACHCA_Leadership_Need_and_Opportunity_Paper_Dana-Olson.pdf

Evashwick, C., & Riedel, J. (2004). *Managing long-term care.* Chicago: AUPHA/HAP.

Havlicek, P. (1999). *Medical group practices in the US: A survey of practice characteristics.* Chicago: American Medical Association.

The Joint Commission. (2008). *Ambulatory care track.* Retrieved November 25, 2008, from http://www.jointcommission.org/AccreditationPrograms/AmbulatoryCare/

Kaiser Family Foundation. (2008). *Prescription drug costs.* Retrieved November 28, 2008, from http://www.kaiseredu.org/topics_im.asp?id=352&imID=1&parentID=68

LA Health Action. (2007). *Safety nets and coverage expansion: ITUP recommendations.* Retrieved November 20, 2008, from http://lahealthaction.org/library/ITUPSafety_nets_and_cove%234305A6.pdf

Liebhaber, A., & Grossman, J. M. (2007, August). *Physicians moving to mid-sized, single-specialty practices.* Tracking Report No. 18 (pp. 1–2). Washington, DC:

Center for Studying Health System Change. Retrieved November 25, 2008, from http://www.hschange.org/CONTENT/941/941.pdf

LongTermCareEducation.com. (n.d.). *Career as an assisted living/Residential care facility administrator.* Retrieved on October 27, 2008, from http://www.longterm careeducation.com/career_paths/career_as_an_assisted_living_r.asp

Managed Care Digest. (n.d.). Retrieved October 27, 2008, from http://www .mcareol.com/factshts/factmco.htm

Medical Group Management Association. (2008a). *American college of medical practice executives personal inventory.* Retrieved November 25, 2008, from http:// www.mgma.com/WorkArea/showcontent.aspx?id=21518

Medical Group Management Association. (2008b). *Body of knowledge for medical practice management.* Retrieved November 25, 2008, from http://www.mgma .com/workarea/showcontent.aspx?id=22924

Milburn, J. B. (2007, January). Mining for gold: Extract revenues from unprocessed claims denials. *MGMA Connexion, 7,* 38–41. Retrieved November 25, 2008, from http://www.sagehealth.com/pdf/Milburn_Cnx07_Jan.pdf

Okie, S. (2008). Innovation in primary care: Staying one step ahead of burnout. *N Engl J Med, 359,* 2305–2309.

PhRMA. (2008). *Key industry facts/About PhRMA.* Retrieved November 28, 2008, from http://www.phrma.org/key_industry_facts_about_phrma/

Pratt, J. R. (1999). *Long-term care: Managing across the continuum.* Gaithersburg, MD: Aspen Publications.

Proenca, E. J., Rosko, M. D., & Dismuke, C. E. (2005). Services collaboration and hospital cost performance: Direct and moderating effects. *Medical Care, 43,* 1250–1258.

Salary.com. (2008). Salary data retrieved November 6, 2008, from http://salary .com/personal/layoutscripts/psnl_default.asp

Seidel, L., Gorsky, R., & Lewis, J. (1995). *Applied quantitative methods for health services management.* Baltimore: Health Professions Press.

Seymour, J. T. (2003). Humanizing health care: Fitness/Wellness centers as the community locus for health promotion. *International Academy for Design and Health.* Retrieved November 23, 2008, from http://www.designandhealth.com/edu_res/ Thomas%20Seymour%20WCDH%202003.pdf

Sharrar, R. G. (1992). General principles of epidemiology. In B. L. Cassens (Ed.), *Preventive medicine and public health: National Medical Series* (2nd ed., p. 2). Baltimore: Williams and Wilkins.

Stone, R. I. (2000, August). *Long-term care for the elderly with disabilities: Current policy, emerging trends, and implications for the twenty-first century.* Retrieved November 25, 2008, from http://www.milbank.org/reports/0008stone/LongTermCare_ Mech5.pdf

Thompson, J. M. (2007). Health services administration. In S. Chisolm (Ed.), *The health professions: Trends and opportunities in U.S. health care* (pp. 357–372). Sudbury, MA: Jones and Bartlett.

Thompson, J. M. (2009). Collaboration in healthcare marketing and business development. In B. Freshman, L. Rubino, & L. Reid-Chassiakos (Eds.), *Collaboration across the disciplines in health care* (pp. 317–344). Sudbury, MA: Jones and Bartlett.

Thompson, J. M., Cockley, D. E., & Bopp, A. E. (2007, Fall). The early career progress of baccalaureate healthcare management students. *The Journal of Health Administration Education, 24,* 359–375.

U.S. Bureau of Labor Statistics. (2007a, December). *Occupational outlook handbook, 2008–09 edition, medical and health services managers.* Retrieved October 18, 2008, from http://www.bls.gov/oco/ocos014.htm

U.S. Bureau of Labor Statistics. (2007b, December). *Career guide to industries, 2008–09 edition, pharmaceutical and medicine manufacturing.* Retrieved November 28, 2008, from http://www.bls.gov/oco/cg/cgs009.htm

U.S. Bureau of Labor Statistics. (2008, March). *Advocacy, grant-making, and civic organizations.* Retrieved November 27, 2008, from http://www.bls.gov/oco/cg/cgs054.htm

U.S. Department of Health and Human Services. (2008a). *HHS: What we do.* Retrieved November 23, 2008, from http://www.hhs.gov/about/whatwedo.html/

U.S. Department of Health and Human Services. (2008b). *Student programs.* Retrieved November 23, 2008, from http://www.hhs.gov/careers/student/index.html

U.S. Department of Health and Human Services. (2008c). *Emerging leaders program (ELP).* Retrieved November 23, 2008, from http://hhsu.learning.hhs.gov/elp/

U.S. Department of Health and Human Services. (2008d). *ELP: Administrative.* Retrieved November 23, 2008, from http://hhsu.learning.hhs.gov/elp/application/administrative.asp

U.S. Office of Personnel Management. (2008). *Salaries and wages: 2008 general schedule (GS) locality pay tables.* Retrieved November 23, 2008, from http://www.opm.gov/oca/08tables/pdf/DCB.pdf

CHAPTER 4

Perspectives from the Field: Profiles of Healthcare Managers

In the previous chapters of this book you learned about the demand for healthcare managers, the education and training required to become a healthcare manager, and the functions carried out by healthcare managers. In addition, you read about the types of settings, both direct and non-direct care, where healthcare managers work. This chapter presents profiles of healthcare managers who currently work in the field and represent a variety of positions, from supervisor/line or staff level to executive/senior management positions, in diverse practice settings. The profiles are based on a structured survey (i.e., each person was asked the same questions), given to healthcare managers who were selected as representative of the wide variety of settings, roles, and functions available in the field.

SAMPLING MATRIX AND PROCESS FOR DEVELOPING PROFILES

"Network" or "snowball" sampling is often used in the "health sciences to investigate rare events or characteristics" (Levy & Lemeshow, 1980, p. 154). The technique is commonly used when a researcher is attempting to find persons "who are likely to know each other" (Vogt, 1993, p. 213). In contrast to random sampling, where a sampling frame is used (e.g., a phone directory or a professional membership directory) and each person has an equal probability of being selected for a survey, we chose to represent specific areas and levels of employment so readers would have a clear sense of what healthcare managers do in a given setting at a particular level of their career. To ensure coverage, we created a matrix and identified the settings we chose to represent in our sample and then located a manager in each setting at supervisor/line or staff, mid-level/director, or executive/senior levels of his or her career.

We chose the following traditional care settings: hospital, nursing homes/skilled nursing facilities, and physician practice. We added recent and established settings: hospital system, retirement community, assisted living, public health, ambulatory clinic/outpatient care, insurer/managed care organization, wellness/fitness, home health, and physical rehabilitation. We also included emerging settings: consulting firm, pharmaceutical firm, professional association, medical supplier, accreditation firm, and government policy/research. We invited 52 healthcare managers to participate; 42 completed the survey, reviewed their profiles, and gave us written permission to publish them. This excellent response rate of 81% was due, in large part, to the strength of our relationships with the participants: alumni of our programs, colleagues in healthcare organizations, preceptors for our student interns, and past coworkers gave generously of their time, expertise, and wisdom. They did this out of a deep commitment to the field of healthcare management and as a gift to future students.

A DAY IN THE LIFE OF HEALTHCARE MANAGERS

The following section provides an overview of how healthcare managers spend their time and use their key skills and abilities, as well as their key sources of satisfaction. Welcome to a day in the life of a healthcare manager!

Proportion of Time Spent on Management Functions

As you learned in Chapter 2, healthcare managers carry out six key management functions: planning, organizing, staffing, controlling, directing, and decision making (Longest, Rakich, & Darr, 2000). As shown in Table 4-1, our 42 survey respondents indicated that they perform all of these functions—in varying proportions.

Table 4-1   Proportion of Time Spent on Each Management Function

Management Function	Proportion of Time Spent on an Average Day				
	0–20%	21–40%	41–60%	61–80%	81–100%
Planning	25.9%	34.9%	16.3%	11.6%	11.7%
Organizing	35.7%	38.1%	11.9%	7.2%	7.1%
Staffing	83.3%	11.9%	2.4%	2.4%	0.0%
Controlling	63.4%	14.6%	7.3%	12.2%	2.4%
Directing	45.2%	30.9%	9.6%	9.5%	4.8%
Decision making	25.6%	37.5%	11.7%	16.3%	7.0%

When you look at what management functions our respondents spent more than 40% of their time on, the order of importance (with respect to time and percent of respondents) was: planning, followed by decision making, organizing, directing, controlling, and staffing. These findings are consistent with the best practices literature that tell us that planning is the most important function of a healthcare manager, and almost 12% of our respondents spent 81–100% of their time on this function.

Use of Knowledge, Skills, and Abilities

When we asked our participants to indicate to what extent they used knowledge, skills, and abilities in their job, they identified speaking clearly and effectively as the top skill they needed and utilized. Table 4-2 provides an overview of the extent to which the respondents use specific types of knowledge, skills, and abilities in descending order of average rating. The **bold** print indicates the largest proportion of responses on the scale.

Thinking back to Chapter 1 and the Healthcare Management Talent Quotient Quiz, does this look familiar? It should, because these are the same knowledge, skills, and abilities (KSAs) that the quiz tapped into. In fact, the top five KSAs, 1) speaking clearly and effectively, 2) thinking critically and analytically, 3) adhering to a professional and ethical code of conduct, 4) working effectively with and motivating others, and 5) writing clearly and effectively, are skills that you can learn and that are taught in high quality HCMN programs. These healthcare managers are reflective and aware of their strengths and what is needed to succeed in their career. When you are looking for HCMN programs, ask about the curriculum, how these KSAs are taught, and how well the program's alumni are doing. You want to find an educational program that teaches all of these KSAs because these are what successful healthcare managers use in their day-to-day work lives. In addition, you want to be sure that there are experiential opportunities such as internships and residencies that enable you to apply your classroom learning to complex real-world problems.

Table 4-2   Extent to Which the Respondents Use Knowledge, Skills, and Abilities

Knowledge, Skill, or Ability	Very Little	Some	Quite a Bit	Very Much	Rating Average
Speaking clearly and effectively	0.0%	0.0%	9.3%	**90.7%**	3.91
Thinking critically and analytically	0.0%	2.3%	16.3%	**81.4%**	3.79
Adhering to a professional and ethical code of conduct	0.0%	4.7%	14.0%	**81.4%**	3.77
Working effectively with and motivating others	0.0%	9.3%	16.3%	**74.4%**	3.65
Writing clearly and effectively	0.0%	9.3%	20.9%	**69.8%**	3.60
Providing leadership to your organization	2.3%	14.0%	16.3%	**67.4%**	3.49
Solving complex and real-world problems	0.0%	14.0%	37.2%	**48.8%**	3.35
Contributing to the welfare of your community	4.8%	23.8%	26.2%	**45.2%**	3.12
Learning effectively on your own	0.0%	14.0%	41.9%	**44.2%**	3.30
Understanding people of other ethnic backgrounds	4.7%	27.9%	32.6%	**34.9%**	2.98
Understanding yourself	2.3%	30.2%	**39.5%**	27.9%	2.93
Analyzing quantitative problems	4.7%	30.2%	**32.6%**	32.6%	2.93

Note. On a scale of 1–4 where 1 = very little and 4 = very much.

Key Sources of Satisfaction

As noted earlier, job satisfaction comes from within and is "a pleasurable or positive emotional state resulting from the appraisal of one's job or job experiences" (Locke, 1983, p. 1300). Table 4-3 provides an overview of our participants' key sources of satisfaction in their positions. Their responses, both rich and varied, are presented here in descending response percentages. Responses greater than 50% are noted with **bold** print.

These responses underscore the fact that teamwork is one of the most important competencies a healthcare manager can have—and the fact that for these respondents, it is one of the top sources of satisfaction in their

Table 4-3   Key Sources of Satisfaction

Source of Satisfaction	Response Percentage
Being a productive member of a team	**81.4%**
Ability to learn and grow in my work	**81.4%**
Helping people and populations through my organization	**76.7%**
Ability to achieve my goals	**76.7%**
The significance of my work	**72.1%**
The high quality of my organization	**72.1%**
Solving complex problems	**65.1%**
Job variety, depth, and breadth	**65.1%**
My colleagues and coworkers	**62.8%**
Positive feedback and rewards for my efforts	**53.5%**
My salary/compensation	**53.5%**
Opportunities for growth and career advancement	**51.2%**
My supportive work environment	**51.2%**
Removing barriers from employees' productivity	46.5%
My organization's excellent reputation	46.5%
Being able to achieve more within my organization than I could outside of it	46.5%
My benefits package	46.5%
The recognition I receive for my work	41.9%
Incentive compensation or bonus	41.9%
Organizational climate	37.2%
Being my own boss	37.2%
Job security	32.6%
My boss	30.2%
Excellent technology and tools for my job	30.2%
Excellent communication in organization	30.2%
Not being tied to a computer all day	25.6%
My commute	25.6%
My job status	20.9%
My office space and office building	16.3%

position. The ability to learn and grow goes hand in hand with solving complex problems; job variety, depth, and breadth; and opportunities for growth and career advancement. Helping people and populations through an organization is another important source of satisfaction. As healthcare managers, we can help people one at a time, or thousands at a time, because we work through something that is larger than us. The high quality of the organization is an important satisfier, as are colleagues, coworkers, and a supportive work environment. Surprisingly, salary, compensation, bonuses, and benefits packages, often the focus of a job search, do not necessarily rank high in key sources of satisfaction. Why not? By reading the profiles of each of the 42 respondents in their own words, perhaps you can find the answer to that question, and the inspiration for your career in healthcare management.

PROFILES OF HEALTHCARE MANAGERS

Each of these profiles has been categorized as to whether the manager's setting is **direct care** or **non-direct care**. Please refer to Chapter 3 for a detailed description of the differences between these two practice settings.

We are deeply indebted to the men and women who responded to our call for participation in this book. These healthcare managers gave freely of their time and of themselves. We truly hope their stories intrigue, uplift, and inspire you.

DIRECT CARE

Larry M. Beck, MBA, MHA, FACHE

President and CEO, The Good Samaritan Hospital of Maryland

Education Completed

Wayne State University, BA, Business Administration, 1971
The George Washington University, MBA, MHA, Healthcare
  Administration, 1974

Fellowship

Administrative Internship, Bon Secours Hospital, Baltimore, Maryland,
1973/74

Certification and Licensure

Fellow, the American College of Healthcare Executives (FACHE)

How First Became Interested in Healthcare Management

When I worked in housekeeping at Hutzel Hospital in Detroit, I was promoted to supervisor of the evening shift. I was 19 years old with responsibility for 45 employees. Then, while attending Wayne State University full
time and working full time, I was mentored by the president of Hutzel
Hospital to continue my education at George Washington University for
graduate school.

Events That Influenced Career

My early leadership experience in housekeeping and mentoring by the
president of Hutzel Hospital influenced my career.

Examples of Decisions Made

Budgetary approvals; program development decisions for new programs
such as assisted living, new office building, expansion of hospital capacity,
infant care, renal services, and so on.

Sources of Satisfaction

My major source of satisfaction is providing health care to 200,000 "moms and dads" each year, with excellent service and quality.

Professional Challenges

Financial challenges; manpower shortages; government intervention and regulation.

Proudest Moment as a Healthcare Manager

I am proud of achieving tremendous growth for Good Samaritan Hospital, building a "World Class" leadership team; enjoying world class Service Excellence Scores and Quality Scorecards.

Career Goals

I plan to continue to leverage all that I have learned to benefit those whom we serve.

Growth Sectors of the Industry for Healthcare Management

Nursing leadership

Professional Role Models and Mentors

Early on, the president of Hutzel Hospital was my role model and mentor. Along the way, hospital executives coached and mentored me. Currently my mentors are my boss, Ken Samet, president of MedStar Health; Harry Rider, president of Union Memorial Hospital; Quint Studer, founder and CEO, Studer Institute; and Al Stubblefield, CEO, Baptist Health Care of Pensacola, Florida.

Knowledge, Skills, Abilities, and Experiences for the Next Generation of Managers

I highly recommend *Hardwiring Excellence* by Quint Studer (2003), along with extensive hands-on and leadership experience.

Advice to Students Desiring to Be Future Managers

Gain related work experience while in school; seek progressive experience in leadership positions.

DIRECT CARE

Michael C. Boblitz, MBA

Director of Planning, Upper Chesapeake Health System

Education Completed

James Madison University, BS, Health Services Administration, 2000
Virginia Commonwealth University, MBA, 2007

How First Became Interested in Healthcare Management

I have a long family history of employment in the healthcare field that sparked my interest to work in the healthcare industry.

Events That Influenced Career

Making an employment change from a position focused primarily on physician practice operations and management to a position that focused on supporting the strategy and business development activities of a hospital has helped to influence my career track.

Examples of Decisions Made

Identify how much additional capacity (e.g., beds, inpatient services, outpatient services, etc.) the organization needs to be prepared to fund and implement over the next 10 years, and develop a timeline of when key events need to occur to ensure new capacity is operational given the projections. Design the budget for six ambulatory programs for FY 2009 that includes staffing/salary requirements ($2.1 million capital budget, and $4 million projected net present value over the first 5 years of operations). As chair of an ambulatory program development task force, I facilitate decision making on course of direction and focal areas to ensure growth targets are achieved. There is significant variation in my day-to-day decision making due to my position.

Professional Challenges

Staying abreast; understanding and forecasting how health care will change in the future.

Proudest Moment as a Healthcare Manager

Several come to mind: (1) I created a late-payment model that resulted in an insurance settlement of over $200,000 related to invoices paid in violation of the Fair Business Practices Act for a faculty practice plan; (2) Being asked to deliver a state-of-the-union/market assessment presentation to the 70 vice presidents, managers, and directors of Martha Jefferson Hospital (at age 27); (3) As an individual, identified a business development opportunity to increase market share in the secondary service area and convinced senior leadership and board of directors to approve and implement the project; (4) Have published articles that appeared on the cover of the American Medical Group Association Group Practice Journal (May 2005), as well as in the Healthcare Financial Management Association Journal (July 2006); and (5) Had the chance to co-instruct a course with Jon Thompson in the Health Services Administration program at James Madison University, and began to learn how academic professors plan for course lectures and assignments.

Career Goals

To become a senior vice president or CEO of a hospital or health system is a career goal of mine.

Growth Sectors of the Industry for Healthcare Management

Performance improvement as it relates to quality. I see great opportunities for management engineers, with responsibility for streamlining operational processes to minimize costs in a world of decreasing reimbursement.

Professional Role Models and Mentors

My father and Tom Girton convinced me to start my own consulting company. Elliot Kuida, COO, Mike Burris, CFO, and Jim Haden, CEO, all at Martha Jefferson Hospital, all took time to help me mature as a healthcare executive and included me in meetings and discussions that expanded my knowledge and experiences. Dean Kaster, my boss and SVP at Upper Chesapeake Health System, has given me responsibilities for high-level projects that I feel that I would not have had the chance to manage at other organizations. Jon Thompson continually pushes me to do more in the healthcare field, and always takes time to advise me on issues as they arise throughout my career. My boss is a great mentor that I work with now. Jon Thompson continues to keep in touch with me and provides advice as needed.

Knowledge, Skills, Abilities, and Experiences for the Next Generation of Managers

Significant analytical competency, including skills in Microsoft Access, will be essential for the next generation of healthcare managers. As health care becomes more competitive, there is an increased need for business and competitive analyses to ensure organizational success.

Advice to Students Desiring to Be Future Managers

Have strong analytical capabilities, and get as many volunteer and internship experiences as possible prior to entering the workforce.

DIRECT CARE

Sandy Cave, RN, BSN
Senior Practice Manager, Fairfax Family Practice

Education Completed
George Mason University, BSN, 1977

Education in Progress
Considering starting a masters in Information Technology (IT) next year; not sure of the school yet.

Certification and Licensure
Registered Nurse (RN)

How First Became Interested in Healthcare Management
After I became president of the Nurses Union while working as a hospital nurse, I was recruited to management when an opening became available in administration. I became president of the nurses union while working for a large Washington-based HMO. It was a position that taught me a great deal about management and employee/management relations. I was recruited to management when an opening became available in administration, and I had a great mentor.

Events That Influenced Career
I had several great mentors when doing nursing union negotiations, as well as the administrator who offered me my first management job. We were always working toward an improved work environment.

Examples of Decisions Made
Human resources decisions on serious matters; IT decisions in conjunction with the IT director; management decisions related to organizational policy; and financial decisions related to the budget are all examples of daily management decisions.

Sources of Satisfaction

I work for a great organization that is always challenging and provides an academic environment, so things are constantly changing.

Professional Challenges

The speed to keep up with healthcare changes and information overload while managing an innovative practice. Trying to keep staff from becoming hardened to patients and burned out, and treating each patient as an individual, are also challenges.

Proudest Moment as a Healthcare Manager

My proudest moment came as the union president, negotiating contracts successfully and working with a federal mediator; successfully building the business from the ground after disengaging from a hospital system.

Career Goals

I want to obtain my master's degree.

Growth Sectors of the Industry for Healthcare Management

Managing information systems and managing change are two areas of growth for future healthcare managers.

Professional Role Models and Mentors

Director of operations, the president of the nurses union prior to me, and my previous boss have all been my role models.

Knowledge, Skills, Abilities, and Experiences for the Next Generation of Managers

Human resources (HR), HR, HR knowledge! IT skills and knowledge, change management, and team development knowledge and skills are all required areas for future managers.

Advice to Students Desiring to Be Future Managers

Spend time learning what the field is about and understanding the demands on healthcare managers.

NON-DIRECT CARE

Stephanie Chisolm, PhD

Director of Education Programs, American Urological
Association Foundation

Education Completed

Hood College, BS, Home Economics/Family Studies, 1981
Rhode Island College, MEd, Health Education, 1990
University of Alabama, PhD, Health Education/Health Promotion, 2000

How First Became Interested in Healthcare Management

I have always been involved in health care, since my first job working first
as a volunteer and then in the food service department at a hospital in high
school.

Events That Influenced Career

My first exposure to health education came during childbirth education
classes 28 years ago. I loved teaching! Women's health and human sexual-
ity issues have always been a personal passion. I spent 6 years in Rhode
Island teaching for a major women's hospital before going to graduate
school to earn my PhD in Health Education/Health Promotion.

Examples of Decisions Made

As the director of education and programs for a national charitable health
organization, budgeting, marketing, and programmatic decisions are all
examples of daily decisions I make.

Sources of Satisfaction

Being able to achieve more as a part of my organization than I could outside of it is a tremendous source of personal satisfaction for me. I hear
from professionals as well as patients and caregivers that the information
and resources we have available help them learn about their urologic diseases and become informed consumers of healthcare services.

Professional Challenges

There are too many worthwhile projects and not enough staff (only two) to accomplish everything. Funding is limited and the need for health information is great. Working with budget constraints presents the challenge to achieve excellence in program and product, on a shoestring.

Proudest Moment as a Healthcare Manager

My proudest moments were when I had a couple of journal publications and completed a textbook and a trade book for patients. Implementing a national health promotion campaign and receiving feedback as a result is also very gratifying.

Career Goals

Continue what I do to the best of my ability, which includes targeting efforts to those that need specific health information and raising awareness about prevention, early diagnosis, and treatment.

Growth Sectors of the Industry for Healthcare Management

Health promotion and disease prevention efforts are cost effective and go a long way to improve the health of individuals across the board. As our population lives longer with each generation, elder care and other gerontology issues will continue to need creative and compassionate professionals to deliver care to the elderly.

Professional Role Models and Mentors

Many nurses have been role models for me professionally. They have provided examples of creative caring and compassion while addressing the physical and mental health of individuals with illness or those that love them. There are often many individuals you may interact with personally and professionally that leave a positive impression on you through their words and actions. There is often opportunity to learn from those individuals and apply those traits to your work.

Knowledge, Skills, Abilities, and Experiences for the Next Generation of Managers

The next generation of managers will need flexibility and customer service skills. There are too many attitudes and not enough caring in health care. We all struggle to do more with less (e.g., less time, less reimbursement) but the consumers (patients) are the ones who suffer because many times professionals lack patience.

Advice to Students Desiring to Be Future Managers

Interacting with individuals when they or a loved one are ill creates many challenges, but many more rewards. They may be stressed, in pain, or even dying. Acting with respect, compassion, and caring will always trump callousness when interacting with others in every situation.

NON-DIRECT CARE

Kristi Donovan, MS, CAE

Associate Director, Education, National Association
of Children's Hospitals and Related Institutions

Education Completed

Towson University, BS, Healthcare Management and Business
    Administration, 1997
Johns Hopkins University, Carey Business School, Master's Degree,
    Organization Development and Strategic Human Resources, 2008

Certification and Licensure

Certified Association Executive (CAE)

How First Became Interested in Healthcare Management

I worked in two mental health programs and a hospice program during
college and really enjoyed the field.

Events That Influenced Career

I've had a few leaders who have been very focused on association management as a career path, and when I saw what can be accomplished through
associations I embraced it.

Examples of Decisions Made

Some examples of decisions are determining how educational programs
will get presented; hotel selection; and determining how we will meet
learning needs of members.

Sources of Satisfaction

In my current position, my greatest satisfaction is derived from supporting members who are taking care of our sickest children. I enjoy the opportunity to serve as a productive member of several organizational teams, as
well. I often have to create my own learning and growth opportunities, but
I do gain a great deal of energy from them.

Professional Challenges

Right now, it's finding growth opportunities in my present organization without having to leave.

Proudest Moment as a Healthcare Manager

Several of my proudest moments involve the relaunch or revitalization of organizational products: a website, a book, and a conference learning guide.

Career Goals

I want to become more involved in the development of organizational culture and strategic planning.

Growth Sectors of the Industry for Healthcare Management

We expect to see a massive turnover in children's hospital leadership and executive level positions.

Professional Role Models and Mentors

Two role models that come to mind: a former CEO and a former boss. The CEO encouraged me to become involved in the American Society of Association Executives (ASAE), which has become a significant resource for me for knowledge and the development of relationships with others in the field. A former boss taught me a great deal about organizational politics and leadership as a woman, probably more through observation and modeling than anything else, but she has continued to be a resource for me in these areas.

Knowledge, Skills, Abilities, and Experiences for the Next Generation of Managers

Communication, enthusiasm, willingness, and expectation to continue to learn; and the ability to write is critical.

Advice to Students Desiring to Be Future Managers

Join your professional association—whatever it is—and get involved. You can learn so much from the professional networks available and make real, lasting change in the profession.

DIRECT CARE

Teresa L. Edwards, MHA, FACHE

Executive Vice President, Bon Secours St. Francis Medical Center

Education Completed

James Madison University, BS, 1980
Virginia Commonwealth University, MHA, 1984

Certification and Licensure

Fellow, American College of Healthcare Executives (FACHE)
Certified Medical Practice Executive (CMPE)

How First Became Interested in Healthcare Management

I was very interested in business, but wanted to work in a business where I felt I added value. Healthcare management is an opportunity to create a better environment for other people and patients.

Events That Influenced Career

Two key factors influenced me: shadowing a healthcare executive while I was in college, and the desire to be a business leader in a position to make improvements.

Examples of Decisions Made

Service expansion, working with physicians to construct and expand services, improving quality of services offered, hospital growth and planning for growth are all examples of decisions I make as an administrator.

Sources of Satisfaction

Continually learning and growing in a changing healthcare environment, working with physicians on solutions which benefit patients, working with other leaders and our community to improve care of the patients we serve, developing other leaders to higher levels of performance, and mentoring young leaders. These all provide me with a great sense of job satisfaction.

Professional Challenges

These are some of the professional challenges I face: system-based rapid change, the need to prioritize time and focus, continually improving the services and financial performance of those services so that additional funds can be invested to improve services.

Proudest Moment as a Healthcare Manager

Opening day of the new hospital was the proudest moment for me as a healthcare manager!

Career Goals

I look forward to using my skills to grow at a larger hospital or have broader geographic or service responsibility in a market.

Growth Sectors of the Industry for Healthcare Management

Nursing and clinical leadership, and physician leadership

Professional Role Models and Mentors

My mother is a role model for me. She was a hard worker and always did her best in every position she held. She was trustworthy and honest. My former boss, Steve Lindsey, has influenced me for over 25 years, was a very effective leader and a man of integrity and ethics.

Knowledge, Skills, Abilities, and Experiences for the Next Generation of Managers

Innovation, flexibility, integrity, and resilience are all important skills for the next generation of managers.

Advice to Students Desiring to Be Future Managers

Seek a good mentor and learn from him or her. Never consider a job to be beneath you. Look for opportunities to learn and grow. Be patient. A career is most successful when you are passionate about it. Choose to pursue something you love!

NON-DIRECT CARE

Christopher Fanning, MHSA

Vice President of Sales and Marketing, Southern Health Services Inc.

Education Completed

Michigan State University, BS, Psychology, 1983
University of Michigan, MHSA, 2000

How First Became Interested in Healthcare Management

I had been in sales management in a different industry and found health-care sales appealing.

Events That Influenced Career

The most significant event was having my vice president discuss with me the idea of graduate education, and encouraging me to go back to school 16 years after I completed my undergraduate degree. As he and I discussed, I was relatively new to the industry and it was clear that I would need additional education to continue moving forward. The best decision I ever made was attending the MHSA program at the University of Michigan.

Examples of Decisions Made

Client relations, personnel, product (benefit) designs, and distribution issues are all things I have to make decisions about on a daily basis.

Professional Challenges

In my position, the challenges are no different than those facing other businesses. Sales, retention, and profitability challenge me just as much as they challenge any other manager in a business.

Growth Sectors of the Industry for Healthcare Management

Provider reimbursement

Knowledge, Skills, Abilities, and Experiences for the Next Generation of Managers

Analytical thinking and progressive thinking are clearly needed in the next generation of managers. Health care is a dynamic industry that is under tremendous financial strain. Adjustments will need to be made to the current system as well as how managers view the healthcare delivery system. Managers that can and are willing to embrace change will be the most successful.

NON-DIRECT CARE

Valerie Fearns

Reimbursement Analyst, Fundamental

Education Completed

Towson University, BS, Health Care Management, 2006

Education in Progress

Towson University, MS, Health Science, concentration in
  Administration, expected graduation date, 2009

How First Became Interested in Healthcare Management

I gained an interest in the field of healthcare management (HCMN) by
working in a local hospital over a summer break. While my original interest was in nursing, it was there I learned the value of becoming a healthcare manager. I worked closely with the nursing staffing office, as well as
the infection control/the Joint Commission department. This experience
provided me with an opportunity to explore career options within the field
of HCMN. It also opened my eyes to a highly valuable occupation in the
healthcare field other than direct care nursing: management. While managers oftentimes take a backseat to licensed professionals such as RNs and
MDs in the field, their worth is invaluable.

Events That Influenced Career

While life is a collection of events, I believe strongly that my undergraduate internship allowed me to be in the position that I currently have. The
required HCMN internship is a semester-long, full-time commitment to
a healthcare company. By developing my relationships with colleagues at
Fundamental I was able to gain full-time employment after graduation. In
time, that position and the mark I was able to leave on the company has
afforded me the opportunity to work with the reimbursement department
as an analyst.

Examples of Decisions Made

In rate analysis, the decision must be made to raise or lower the rates of patients in order to gain the maximum reimbursement. Another decision that is common in my position is accepting or declining bad debt logs from the facilities. A lot of my responsibilities vary day to day, so the decisions may change as well.

Sources of Satisfaction

As a young professional in the field, I truly felt the only reward would come through my salary—but I was wrong. Although salary is important, it is not the most satisfying. The satisfactions of being able to solve unique problems and being praised for my efforts are priceless. Full job satisfaction comes from being with an organization that applauds hard work and welcomes opportunities for growth to qualified individuals.

Professional Challenges

One of the biggest challenges I face is the complexity of balancing business and the emotional connection to patients. Having been exposed to the financial aspects solely, it is hard to step away from the "bottom line" mindset that I have. It is hard to look at patients as a paycheck, and while care is always intended to be the forefront of priorities, sadly enough it is not always the case in real life. Health care is a big business that profits from patients' needs. Having a balance between a business mindset and compassion is often difficult.

Proudest Moment as a Healthcare Manager

My proudest moment in HCMN was being able to collect over $70,000 in reimbursement from Medicaid due to inaccurate collection efforts. After performing an account analysis on several departments and cost centers, I recognized multiple miscodings. The identification of those miscodings allowed Fundamental to re-collect and obtain over $70,000 in reimbursement that was originally rejected.

Career Goals

As a young professional, I have many goals and aspirations for my HCMN career. With an anticipated graduation with my MS in Health Science in

2009, I hope to have increased job opportunities. One position of partic-ular interest to me is that of a health policy analyst for the government. With my experience and my MS, I hope to achieve the goal of acquiring this position. Also, prior to graduation I would like to become a Certified Health Education Specialist (CHES). My long-term goals include going back to school to receive a PhD in Public Health and possibly teaching or working in the not-for-profit sector of health care.

Growth Sectors of the Industry for Healthcare Management

Long-term care will definitely be a growth sector. With the aging of the baby boomers, there will be an increased need for managers in nursing homes, rehabilitation facilities, and hospice. The new generation of health-care managers, including myself, will most certainly have job security in that particular sector.

Professional Role Models and Mentors

My professional role models in the field are my advisors—both at the undergraduate and graduate levels, then and now. Both undergraduate and graduate advisors have taught me in and out of the classroom. Their expertise went beyond the walls of the classroom, and they were able to advise me along the way. Knowing they were experienced professionals in the field, I sought their advice prior to making any major career decisions. They have influenced me and reassured me that no task is unachievable. Without their advice I might not be back in school pursuing my goal of obtaining my MS.

Knowledge, Skills, Abilities, and Experiences for the Next Generation of Managers

The next decade of HCMN colleagues will need to be driven to succeed in this business. To achieve and obtain a good position in HCMN takes devotion and dedication. Having an excellent education, extending upon it, and being a believer in continuous learning will allow one to succeed. Changes occur constantly in this field; it is important for an individual to be able to adapt quickly to those changes. Those who are knowledgeable, charismatic, and driven will do well in HCMN.

Advice to Students Desiring to Be Future Managers

I would advise those considering a career in healthcare management to go back to school and receive a master's degree in the field. I personally feel that the field is moving in the direction of requiring this degree. Many positions I have seen often require, if not, desire individuals to have a master's degree. I know that through the experience of returning to school, I have been able to increase my professional network and increase my worth to the field. It also provides individuals with an opportunity to see what other positions fellow healthcare managers have. The experience is truly unique and extends any education and training one might have received at the undergraduate level.

DIRECT CARE

William J. Forbes, PhD

Director, Wellness Center and Baltimore County Department of Aging
Senior Fitness Project, Towson University

Education Completed

Loch Haven University, BS, Health Education, 1966
University of Pittsburgh, MA, Exercise Physiology, 1967
University of Maryland, PhD, Exercise Physiology/Zoology, 1990

Certification and Licensure

Cardiopulmonary Resuscitation (CPR)
Advanced Cardiovascular Life Support (ACLS)

How First Became Interested in Healthcare Management

I came to healthcare management later in my career with my involvement
in cardiac rehabilitation.

Events That Influenced Career

Working on my PhD dissertation (1987–1990), which dealt with the
effects of exercise training and antihypertensive medications on training,
really put me on this path.

Examples of Decisions Made

Some examples of decisions I make include review of medical files and subsequent entry and risk stratification of cardiac patients and senior fitness
participants; equipment purchase and repairs; spending and budget decisions; staff management decisions; staff scheduling; program scheduling;
fitness/health risk-assessment decisions; exercise prescriptions for participants; and participant program evaluations.

Sources of Satisfaction

The greatest satisfaction is observing the improvement in health, fitness,
and quality of life of participants in my program. I also enjoy helping
young staff improve their clinical skills and develop as professionals. I have

had the pleasure of observing significant growth and improved quality of programming in my facility over the years.

Professional Challenges

Some of my professional challenges include dealing with 15 direct-report staff, some of whom can be very needy; the multitasking required to deal with nine wellness centers that I direct; not having an administrative assistant and dealing with every detail associated with the job; insufficient time in a 40-hour work week; and consistently having to work overtime.

Proudest Moment as a Healthcare Manager

My proudest moment was when I was elected to president of the National Association for Kinesiology and Physical Education in Higher Education.

Career Goals

My goal at this point in my career is to retire within the next year.

Growth Sectors of the Industry for Healthcare Management

I foresee growth in wellness center management, health club management, and disease prevention programs.

Professional Role Models and Mentors

I have been lucky to have had many. Graduate professors and advisors in exercise physiology mentored me during my graduate work. Physicians with whom I work in cardiac programming have influenced my career by helping to increase my knowledge, passion, and interest in this field.

Knowledge, Skills, Abilities, and Experiences for the Next Generation of Managers

Managers need great people skills; computer technology skills; management skills; excellent clinical skills; good teamwork skills; communication skills, including writing, public speaking, and teaching; and time management skills.

Advice to Students Desiring to Be Future Managers

Develop an excellent foundation of knowledge, people skills, teamwork skills, clinical skills, and management skills. Take advantage of internships/practica to develop clinical skills. Above all, have passion for your job.

NON-DIRECT CARE

Harry Fox

Account Manager, Major Accounts, CareFirst Blue Cross Blue Shield

Education Completed

University of Baltimore, BS, Business Administration with Business Education minor, 1970

Student teacher at Kenwood Senior High School, Social Business Courses, Fall 1969

Certification and Licensure

Health and Life Insurance License

How First Became Interested in Healthcare Management

Bottom line: A major employer who is recognized worldwide, Blue Cross Blue Shield, "helping people" stay well and also at a time of need.

Events That Influenced Career

I have always been client focused and I follow through. Plus I have good communication skills, common sense, and I'm "down to earth."

Examples of Decisions Made

Development of a multimillion-dollar account renewal, introduction of a product to satisfy a need, that is, to reduce healthcare costs, or satisfy a benefit need, and/or suggest a benefit alternative for various reasons.

Sources of Satisfaction

I have a very flexible job with a great staff that reports to me, a real team, and a terrific boss.

Professional Challenges

One of my biggest challenges is renewing existing business in a very competitive environment with rising healthcare costs.

Proudest Moment as a Healthcare Manager

I can't say that there has been just one, but seeing my staff learn and grow is very rewarding.

Career Goals

My goal is to continue to be successful and grow and I may consider retiring within 5 or 6 years.

Growth Sectors of the Industry for Healthcare Management

As a member of the "third-party vendor world," I see more open access, no gatekeeper, but more tools available to educate the consumer to make better decisions as to how, where, and from whom to access/request non-emergency care.

Professional Role Models and Mentors

I have had both good and bad role models. I have learned from both as to how to and what not to do or say. If you are good, you learn from everyone as to what does and what doesn't work in the real world with different clients and large customers.

Knowledge, Skills, Abilities, and Experiences for the Next Generation of Managers

You will need strong computer skills, great analytical skills, and communication skills. Most importantly, you will need outstanding people skills. Good organization and presentation skills are very important, too. Finally, you must have common sense!

Advice to Students Desiring to Be Future Managers

Be prepared to learn a great deal, work hard, and continue to learn. The environment is always changing.

NON-DIRECT CARE

Treg Fuller, MSS

Vice President of Training and Recruitment, MedSource Consultants

Education Completed

Atlantic Christian College, BS, Sports Science, 1988
United States Sports Academy, MSS, 1991

How First Became Interested in Healthcare Management

I was recruited into the role working in physician recruitment.

Events That Influenced Career

Being the first manager in physician recruitment and my initial training in the field set my goals and objectives for my career.

Examples of Decisions Made

Addition of staff to firm, consulting with administrators and hiring authorities within group practices on physician staffing needs, as well as career consultation to physicians looking at making a career change or position change, are all part of my daily decisions.

Professional Challenges

A big challenge is the lack of physicians coming out of training each year compared to the demand for primary care physicians and specialists that are needed. We have a very large problem in the United States with the lack of qualified healthcare providers coming out of training each year.

Proudest Moment as a Healthcare Manager

Recruiting a pediatric cardiac surgeon to Inova Fairfax Hospital for Children was a proud moment for me. There was a huge need in the area and the physician that we recruited is world class, and has brought exceptional care to the area for children in desperate need of his services.

Career Goals

Build MedSource Consultants to be an integrated recruitment solution for health systems, hospitals, and groups in the United States.

Growth Sectors of the Industry for Healthcare Management

Administration, marketing

Professional Role Models and Mentors

Joe Hawkins and Joe Caldwell both influenced the way I saw physician recruitment and the professional nature by which the work can be done.

Knowledge, Skills, Abilities, and Experiences for the Next Generation of Managers

Future managers need to understand the integration of health care, not just how one particular aspect works; managers need to appreciate how each area of healthcare delivery is affected by the others. We have too many people in health care that are specialists in one area, but don't understand that what they do affects the whole healthcare delivery system.

Advice to Students Desiring to Be Future Managers

Get into it only if you love it and love being a part of taking care of people. You have to have the mindset of a physician or nurse without the tools to treat the patients, but the acumen to help the providers care for the patients and care about their families as well.

DIRECT CARE

Schuyler Fury
Administrator, Riverdale Assisted Living Facility

Education Completed
James Madison University, BS, Health Services Administration, 2007

Education in Progress
Liberty University, MBA, expected graduation date, December 2009

Certification or Licensure
Emergency Medical Technician—Basic
Virginia Licensed Medication Aide

How First Became Interested in Healthcare Management
I always had an interest in working in health care since I was in elementary school. My entire life, I had always wanted to be a doctor until my first semester of college when I took premedical chemistry. I decided that I did not want to do that and wanted to become a nurse. During this time, I was working at Alleghany Regional Hospital in the summer and I started to see how the business side of health care worked. So, when I went back to school in the fall and started investigating health services administration (HSA), I decided to use that as a backup if I decided not to do nursing. In the end, I decided against nursing and switched my major to HSA. When I started taking the classes, I realized this was what I really liked doing. By doing HSA, I could still work in health care and do what I was good at which was the business side. Also, I really liked learning about policies and regulation and seeing how health care has evolved.

Events That Influenced Career
When I was working in a previous position at a nursing home, I saw things being done that I did not agree with, such as resident abandonment, abuse, neglect, and multiple poor business and healthcare practices. During that time, I was not in a position to influence change for the better. I started to

get very upset because I could not help to make that place a better place without getting reprimanded. That is when I decided that I wanted to be an advocate for those in long-term care settings and to help make things better for them. I decided not to give up on long-term care, and wanted to find a company that I believed in and that would believe in me and give me the power to make positive changes. When I started with American Retirement Homes, I found just what I wanted and as the administrator for Riverdale, I am responsible for the well-being of my employees and residents. I like being able to enforce the appropriate policies, make changes, and see a positive outcome. Also, in long-term care there is a great opportunity to give back to the elderly who have given so much in their lifetime to the communities that they served. They deserve respect and top-notch care, which in my position, I have the opportunity to make happen.

Examples of Decisions Made

I make admissions decisions as to who is suitable for assisted living care at Riverdale, whether or not to hire or fire someone, when and how to discipline someone, where and whom to market to, and how to best manage a budget.

Sources of Satisfaction

I really like knowing that I have had a positive impact on people and their needs at the end of the day. It is rewarding to have the opportunity to make change for the better and to see a facility grow because of the positive satisfaction that I am able to bring to the facility.

Professional Challenges

The key challenge I face in my specific role is that my company is small and that it competes with major corporations. There is a lot of competition that I am up against in the Charlottesville area. I also face a lot of staffing challenges and ethics challenges as far as staffing and staff policy compliance. Also, there are a lot of people in the professional community who really question my ability to do my job because I am so young. However, once they get to know me and see how I work, they feel more comfortable and have really come to depend on me as another healthcare professional.

Proudest Moment as a Healthcare Manager

Receiving positive feedback from the residents and families of the residents that I serve is always a proud moment for me. Also, gaining respect from my employees, and having them thank me for turning the place around and for giving them someone they can count on, are also proud moments.

Career Goals

I would like to stay at my current position for about 2 to 3 years because the facility is small and I can learn a lot. Once I complete my MBA, I would like to do some research in healthcare policies and maybe work my way into a position as an administrator at a larger facility or as a corporate administrator. I think I would really like being a "clean-up" administrator that goes into problem facilities and straightens out their problems because I enjoy making the needed changes and seeing the outcomes. I would also like to be a state inspector at some point. Down the road, I would like to get my PhD in Business Management and see where that takes me.

Growth Sectors of the Industry for Healthcare Management

Definitely the long-term care sector, because the baby boomers are hitting the facilities and there are not enough healthcare managers and workers to meet the demand.

Professional Role Models and Mentors

One of my role models was Mr. Chip Peal who was the COO at Alleghany Regional Hospital when I worked there, but he is now a CEO at another HCA hospital. He really believed in me and really made me think about healthcare management. He helped me see what I was good at and how I should use my talents. Also, Dr. Jon Thompson, my advisor and professor at JMU, was a huge role model for me. I loved hearing his stories about his career and what he had done in his professional life. He is very intelligent and wise about the healthcare industry, and I would love to be as knowledgeable as him one day. My current mentor is Kim Hurt, who is one of the corporate administrators for American Retirement Homes. She has been a huge influence on me because she has been with the company for 14 years and knows the company inside and out. She is kind, compassionate, and very outgoing. She always gives 100% and is a great teacher and leader by example.

Knowledge, Skills, Abilities, and Experiences for the Next Generation of Managers

They need to be able to absorb as much information as possible. They also need to learn that different people have different work ethics and different goals and they should be able to respect that. It is always great to experience things firsthand in the "field." Therefore, I would tell people to volunteer or work in health care as much as possible while getting their education.

Advice to Students Desiring to Be Future Managers

Never be afraid of change because health care is always changing. Also, learn about each sector of health care, not just one area. It is always good to be able to know a little bit about each sector because they interconnect at various points. I absolutely love what I do! It seemed like it took me a while to get to this point, but it is amazing that I am so young, and am doing what I wanted to do so quickly. I think determination is something one must possess because healthcare management can cause a high rate of burnout, but is very rewarding if one can stay with it.

DIRECT CARE

Theresa C. Honchar, LPN

Health Service Director, Brightview of Mays Chapel

Education Completed

University of Maryland, School of Practical Nursing, 1964

Certification or Licensure

Licensed Practical Nurse (LPN) with License to Practice in Maryland and Virginia

How First Became Interested in Healthcare Management

Under the direction and supervision of very strong and caring associates, I found value in leading others in concepts of good practical care that each of us deserves.

Events That Influenced Career

Strong leadership and weak leadership have all influenced me, as well as the importance of educating caregivers and patients.

Examples of Decisions Made

Daily work schedules, medication administration/ordering medications, physician calls, family calls, assessments for admission or readmission, and discharges are all decisions I have to make daily.

Sources of Satisfaction

The ability to lead, teach, and give our residents a quality of life is a great source of satisfaction for me.

Professional Challenges

Lack of understanding of the concept of assisted living is challenging.

Proudest Moment as a Healthcare Manager

I had a young man who worked in our food services department. He wanted to work in the nursing department for the summer. He was very successful as a resident assistant. He returned to college in the fall. When he returned home after his first semester, he announced that he had changed his major from finance to nursing.

Career Goals

To continue to mentor my staff, and prepare them by providing education in aging, dementia, and related illnesses.

Growth Sectors of the Industry for Healthcare Management

Geriatrics

Professional Role Models and Mentors

I was very fortunate to be introduced to an RN visiting nurse when I was 12 years old. She showed me the excitement of taking care of others. She taught me that compassion comes from the heart, and together with the right knowledge, I could make a difference in the lives of others. She was extremely professional and proud, and I longed to emulate her.

Knowledge, Skills, Abilities, and Experiences for the Next Generation of Managers

Key knowledge and skills include understanding human behavior and how to accept the responsibility of providing quality service to enhance quality of life. Future managers need to be professional, understanding, and self-less.

Advice to Students Desiring to Be Future Managers

Spend time in a healthcare environment. Have a heart. I hope that my 44-year career has touched the lives and minds of people that I have encountered!

DIRECT CARE

Andrew Jones, MS

Vice President, General Services, Edenwald Retirement Community

Education

Towson University, BS, Healthcare Management, 2004
Towson University, MS, Health Science, 2008

Certification and Licensure

Certified Dietary Manager (CDM)

How First Became Interested in Healthcare Management

I have worked in the healthcare field for numerous years and enjoy the interaction with the residents. The prospect of making a difference in the care that the residents receive has been my passion. A thank you and a smile from a resident warm my heart.

Events That Influenced Career

I have worked in the senior living field for 25 years. Realizing that an aging baby boomer population was on the verge of entering the senior living sector, I decided to return to school to obtain my degree in the healthcare management field so that I could pursue my goal of advancing to administrative and management positions in this field. The course offerings and professors at Towson influenced my decision to pursue my MS.

Examples of Decisions Made

Some of the areas I work in and make decisions about include research of cost control measures, regulation compliance, quality assurance program development, budget preparation, inventory control/analysis, and demand/supply forecasting. Depending on the market conditions, decisions are made accordingly along with personnel decisions on hiring and recommending termination. Decisions are made daily on the operational side.

Professional Challenges

Economic factors that can adversely impact the care and services that you can provide to the residents. While government regulation is very important to ensure that the residents receive adequate and proper care sometimes the increased regulations can have an adverse affect on how the staff provides the necessary care to the residents. A changing dynamic in the employee work ethic has affected the care and commitment to the residents and the organization. Generational shifts in the population will force managers to adapt new programs to ensure that the needs of the new clientele are met accordingly. Managers must understand that a balance between the current and new generation must be achieved to satisfy both groups.

Proudest Moment as a Healthcare Manager

My proudest moments were when I received my degrees in healthcare management. The degrees will allow me to pursue my goals. My undergraduate and graduate degrees have developed my managerial, communication, analytical thinking, and research skills.

Career Goals

To hold an upper-management position within a not-for-profit continuing care retirement community (CCRC) or another similar type of industry.

Growth Sectors of the Industry for Healthcare Management

The CCRC industry will continue to grow as the baby boomers enter the marketplace.

Professional Mentors

Sal Molite, president of Edenwald, has allowed me to pursue my goal of attending school. Over the past 17 years he has developed my managerial skills. He has always put the residents' well-being first. Sal allows his managers to manage by using a macro-management approach, instead of micro-managing. He understands the importance of every position within the organization and always listens to the line-level employees for suggestions and input. He understands the changing marketplace and utilizes long range planning strategies to ensure that Edenwald remains competitive in the senior living industry.

Knowledge, Skills, Abilities, and Experiences for the Next Generation of Managers

Managers need to have an understanding of the generational shift in the aging population, along with a comprehensive understanding of the regulatory challenges that they will be facing from increased government oversight. Students must have a comprehensive view of the financial crisis that is looming in the healthcare industry.

Advice to Students Desiring to Be Future Managers

The industry is growing and has many different avenues that one can pursue. Be committed and you can make a difference!

DIRECT CARE

J. S. Parker Jones, IV, MS, CNHA, FACHCA

Administrator, Heritage Hall Nursing and Rehabilitation Center

Education Completed

East Texas State University (now Texas A&M University), BS,
    Psychology and Sociology, 1970
East Texas State University, MS, Counseling and Guidance, 1971

Certification or Licensure

Fellow, American College of Healthcare Administrators (FACHCA)
Certified Nursing Home Administrator (CNHA), American College of
    Nursing Home Administrators

How First Became Interested in Healthcare Management

My parents were physical therapists and a facility that they worked for had
just expanded. The family that owned it needed help with admissions for
both of the two facilities they owned, and I started my career in admissions.

Events That Influenced Career

I had an opportunity in Massachusetts to work in nursing home admissions, and then moved to Virginia for an opportunity as the administrator. After 25 years with one company and change in owners, I decided that
I had had enough. I offered to help Heritage Hall on an interim basis for
6 to 8 weeks until they were able to find an administrator. After a couple
of months, I was offered the opportunity to stay and I have been here
nearly 9 years.

Professional Challenges

It is difficult to have the reimbursement keep pace with increased wage
expense associated with having adequate staff. As acuity of residents
increases, our need for increased numbers and competency of staff grows.

Also, it is challenging trying to get the community to understand that the healthcare system cannot cure everyone and everything. Facilities and staff are not the "bad guys."

Proudest Moment as a Healthcare Manager

When the residents and families say "thank you."

Career Goals

To continue to get good state survey results and continue with the development of programs that enhance resident satisfaction.

Growth Sectors of the Industry for Healthcare Management

Growth of nursing homes and assisted living facilities, as well as licensure of assisted living administrators and the focus on more regulation, will create a huge void. There is also high turnover of nursing home administrators, as we are beaten up over survey results by the state, corporate offices, and the health professions. Opportunities in long-term care are excellent.

Professional Role Models and Mentors

Luis Warf, retired CEO, provided an opportunity to learn by example and experience. In difficult times, he did not "throw the baby out with the bath." He stuck with his personnel and got positive return for his investment and confidence in staff. Also, the regional operations VP of my company and the vice president of clinical services serve as role models. During times when I get tunnel vision on an issue, they help broaden my perspective by increasing my options based on experiences they have had in other facilities.

Knowledge, Skills, Abilities, and Experiences for the Next Generation of Managers

They will need a strong work ethic, communication skills, and the opportunity to work in long-term care and to be exposed to the duties of each department and how they interact. Also, future managers need a good understanding of the reimbursement processes for Medicare, Medicaid, and insurance.

Advice to Students Desiring to Be Future Managers

Be patient, consistent, fair with staff, and adaptable to daily issues.

NON-DIRECT CARE

Michael Jurgensen, MHA

Senior Vice President, Health Policy and Planning, The Medical Society of Virginia

Education Completed

Manatee Junior College, AS, Respiratory Therapy, 1981
James Madison University, BS, Public Administration, 1983
Medical College of Virginia, Virginia Commonwealth University, MHA, 1986

How First Became Interested in Healthcare Management

A combination of previous clinical/allied health experiences and completion of a Public Administration degree contributed to my interest in healthcare management.

Events That Influenced Career

Personal interest, academic choices, varied experience in healthcare sectors, and happenstance. Also, I read Paul Starr's *The Social Transformation of American Medicine* when it was first released, which was very influential.

Examples of Decisions Made

Policy and political decisions, lobbying, regulatory and legislative initiatives to be pursued, and positions the organization will take on issues are all decisions I address daily.

Professional Challenges

Gaining consensus and/or developing strategies on a wide variety of healthcare issues among a professional association membership that is extremely diverse in their opinions as well as their individual expectations and levels of political and policy sophistication.

Career Goals

Continuing to grow with and contribute to my current organization are personal goals.

Growth Sectors of the Industry for Healthcare Management

We will need primary care providers of all types who are able to respond to the healthcare needs of an aging population.

Knowledge, Skills, Abilities, and Experiences for the Next Generation of Managers

Common sense, clear understanding of the reasons why we are in health care, and the foresight and ingenuity necessary to move our healthcare system forward will be necessary for the next generation of managers.

Advice to Students Desiring to Be Future Managers

Be prepared to be challenged, be certain you can face complexity, and know that you are able to deal with people of varied educational, income, and power levels.

DIRECT CARE

Sharon E. Kelley, RN, MS, NEA-BC

Vice President for Patient Care Services and Chief Nurse Executive, Mt. Washington Pediatric Hospital

Education Completed

LPN Diploma, 1969
Essex Community College, AA Nursing, 1975
College of Notre Dame, BSN, 1983
University of Maryland, MS, Nursing Administration, 1985
Wharton School of Business, University of Pennsylvania, Executive Fellow, 2006

Certification and Licensure

Nurse Executive Advanced, Board Certified (NEA-BC)

How First Became Interested in Healthcare Management

Very early in my career I felt there was so much more I could contribute to the bigger picture and longed to have the most significant impact on the quality of patient care that I could. It was my passion to lead in this field.

Events That Influenced Career

Seeing the need for change and knowing that if I set upon the course I could make it happen, and experiencing improved patient outcomes and healing.

Examples of Decisions Made

Negotiation in difficult situations; reallocating resources; setting policy and standards for practice; and resolving problems that others have given up on by making tough decisions.

Sources of Satisfaction

Making a difference in the lives of others. The incredible team I have built. We have made significant improvements in departmental operations, have had a very positive impact on the bottom line, and elevated clinical practice through multidisciplinary management.

Professional Challenges

Cost constraints and reduction in reimbursement; little opportunity for growth within; workforce shortages; generational changes in work ethic; partnering with physicians in patient safety.

Proudest Moment as a Healthcare Manager

On occasions in different positions, I was highly effective in turning around operations with very positive patient and organizational outcomes. One of my proudest and most fulfilling moments as a clinician was the first cardiac arrest patient I worked on with the team. I watched the patient recover and go home with his family. As a manager, it was the first time I was able to rally and motivate an interdisciplinary team to totally redesign the emergency department patient-flow process, which sent satisfaction scores soaring and watched them celebrate the difference they make.

Career Goals

Perhaps a doctorate or a COO role. In any regard, I want to be the best that I can be in giving back and contribute to the development of the next generation of healthcare managers.

Growth Sectors of the Industry for Healthcare Management

Outpatient services and care of the elderly

Professional Role Models and Mentors

Strong, effective, and ethical women who earned their way up the ladder, making no excuses and demonstrating success.

Knowledge, Skills, Abilities, and Experiences for the Next Generation of Managers

Passion for excellence, commitment to the patients and healing, the ability to walk a mile in their shoes, critical thinking and sound judgment, a business sense, more and better clinical training, effective and timely decision making, and assertiveness to do the right thing, always.

Advice to Students Desiring to Be Future Managers

It's an admirable venture. Give it the best of you. Your focus must be on the care of others in an effective and efficient manner. You will accomplish what you make a focused commitment to.

NON-DIRECT CARE

Mary Beth Kiser, MPH

Manager, Health Plan Employer Data and Information Set (HEDIS) Policy, National Committee for Quality Assurance

Education Completed

James Madison University, BS, Health Services Administration, 2000
George Washington University, MPH, Health Policy, 2008

How First Became Interested in Healthcare Management

I had served in a variety of capacities prior to my managing projects/deliverables, and it was the next logical step in my professional career.

Events That Influenced Career

Having experienced a number of positions prior to management, I was exposed to team dynamics and various management styles. I learned from these dynamics and ultimately wanted to demonstrate my unique management capabilities—specifically, process improvement.

Examples of Decisions Made

Verification of written customer service responses by fellow staff and process improvement for a more user-friendly publication are examples of daily decisions.

Professional Challenges

Staff turnover is often high, leading to disruptions in work flow and challenges with new employee learning curves. Indifferent management styles or attitudes have also been challenging at times, but I've learned from these and understand how to counter such styles in order to work effectively in team settings.

Proudest Moment as a Healthcare Manager

Continuous process and product improvement, as it relates to the usability of the Healthcare Effectiveness Data and Information Set (HEDIS) specification publication.

Career Goals

I seek to continue my role in project management, including management of larger teams. I am particularly interested in the ways health information technology will continue to improve our healthcare delivery system, and I look forward to taking part in this movement, be it from an advocacy or policy standpoint, or in a more direct, implementation capacity.

Professional Role Models and Mentors

Supervisors and former academic professors serve as my role models. I have learned from their leadership styles and industry expertise. These colleagues have helped shape me into a more informed, effective, and confident professional.

Knowledge, Skills, Abilities, and Experiences for the Next Generation of Managers

The next generation of managers should have effective communication skills (written and verbal), project management skills, and a working knowledge of the U.S. healthcare system. As the field gets more competitive, it will be critical to distinguish yourself from your peers. There are a number of ways you may do this, and it will take time for you to understand those strengths on which to capitalize and weaknesses to be improved.

Advice to Students Desiring to Be Future Managers

Networking should be on your weekly task list. This has helped open many professional doors for me, and it will prove essential to you. Continuous education is another driver. This could entail taking classes, attending seminars, or simply keeping abreast of current healthcare industry news.

DIRECT CARE

Lauren Koontz

Research Analyst II, Baltimore City Health Department

Education Completed

Towson University, BS, Healthcare Management, 2001

Education in Progress

Johns Hopkins School of Public Health, Master of Public Health
Program, expected date of completion May 2009

How First Became Interested in Healthcare Management

I first found out about the Healthcare Management program through a
friend at Towson University. I was actually enrolled as an economics major
and was not sure this was the best fit for me. Healthcare Management
seemed like a promising career path. It turned out I enjoyed my Healthcare Management and Health Science courses a great deal.

Events That Influenced Career

I found that working in the hospital or doctor's office setting did not
inspire or satisfy me. Traveling abroad piqued my interest in the broader,
"big-picture" field of public health and policy. I felt I could have a bigger
impact on healthcare service delivery by pursuing a career in public health.

Examples of Decisions Made

Decisions I make typically include recommendations for changes in health
service delivery, program initiatives or funding, which are based on health
services research.

Sources of Satisfaction

The most satisfying aspects of my present position include the opportunities for growth I have experienced. Also satisfying to me is the flexibility to
work on projects that I have envisioned or designed, and the importance

I feel my work plays in the lives of low-income individuals who may have few resources.

Professional Challenges

Challenges include changes in the mandates associated with federal funding for programs and encouraging or facilitating meaningful improvement across the healthcare field.

Proudest Moment as a Healthcare Manager

My proudest moment was when I began a new initiative/project at work and felt that I really started a new direction or capacity for the department.

Career Goals

Some of my short-term goals include completing my MPH, finishing a research project, and publishing a journal article.

Growth Sectors of the Industry for Healthcare Management

I see growth in the need for data management and evaluation skills. While this may be more applicable to the public health field, I think more and more decisions are being made based on data and outcome measures.

Knowledge, Skills, Abilities, and Experiences for the Next Generation of Managers

Flexibility is a must; changes are frequent in the healthcare field. Depending on the specific area of interest, I think understanding budgets and financial management is key, as is an understanding of statistics.

Advice to Students Desiring to Be Future Managers

I would recommend volunteering in the area of interest. This kind of exposure to the "real world" can clarify your interests and impact your decision about your future career.

DIRECT CARE

Jim Krauss, MHSA, FACHE

President and CEO, Rockingham Memorial Hospital

Education Completed

Pennsylvania State University, BA, General Arts and Sciences, 1980
George Washington University, MHSA, 1986

Certification or Licensure

Fellow, American College of Healthcare Executives (FACHE)

How First Became Interested in Healthcare Management

I had a need to do something in my life that would benefit others and
improve the community in which I lived.

Events That Influenced Career

Serving as a healthcare extentionist with the Peace Corps, I found health
care to be personally rewarding. I continued to pursue international
healthcare opportunities until I concluded that constant travel would not
be conducive to raising a family. A close friend worked in the U.S. Surgeon
General's Office and was able to arrange an interview for me with Dr.
Koop. Through that discussion I decided to pursue administrative positions within the U.S. healthcare system, targeting hospital management.

Examples of Decisions Made

Some examples of decisions I make include deciding which issues to take
to the board, changes to make in annual strategic and tactical plans, management structure, resolution of concerns arising from the construction of
the replacement hospital, business arrangements with third parties, inter-
face with officials, and how to involve the medical staff in improving care.

Professional Challenges

Being visible in a large organization, finding enough time to accomplish important things, covering all the internal political bases, and determining what we are not going to do are all challenges in my role.

Proudest Moment as a Healthcare Manager

Seeing clinicians achieve goals they thought they could not achieve in clinical programs.

Career Goals

My goal is to transition the local healthcare delivery system to best meet the future needs of the community.

Growth Sectors of the Industry for Healthcare Management

Ambulatory care is a high growth area for the profession.

Professional Role Models and Mentors

The president of the hospital where I completed my residency had an influence on my career path. The president was my preceptor and he allowed me to participate in the most confidential of details in running a health system. He kept a high energy level going with the executive staff resulting in high performance. I learned that his key to success was surrounding himself with talented people and then letting them do their work without interference. My residency preceptor taught me enduring lessons.

Knowledge, Skills, Abilities, and Experiences for the Next Generation of Managers

They will need to know how the healthcare delivery system is different from other industries. They will need to be skilled at problem solving and leadership. They will need experiences within health care stemming from volunteering, fellowships, and then working their way up to ever increasing levels of responsibility.

Advice to Students Desiring to Be Future Managers

Select a master's program with a residency or fellowship program.

DIRECT CARE

Amanda Llewellyn, MHA/MBA, FACHE

Assistant Administrator, Ambulatory Services and Clinical Operations, Johns Hopkins Health System

Education Completed

University of Maryland University College, BA, Business
   Administration, 2005
University of Maryland University College, MHA, 2006
University of Maryland University College, MBA, 2008

Certification and Licensure

Fellow, American College of Healthcare Executives (FACHE)
Fellow, Association of Healthcare Resource and Materials Management
   (FAHRMM)
Certified Purchasing Manager (CPM)
Certified Materials and Resource Professional (CMRP)

Education in Progress

University of Maryland University College, Doctorate of Management
   Program

How First Became Interested in Healthcare Management

With a single mother in healthcare management, we spent the summers working in the hospital as volunteers. I was interested in clinical areas, and was often asked by the faculty if I would be a nurse someday. However, my talents were in the analytical and business aspects of the organization. Those abilities enabled me to work through my degrees and placed me on a path to healthcare administration. It was definitely in our blood.

Events That Influenced Career

Both personal and professional events shaped my journey into healthcare administration. Having married young and working two jobs, it was more difficult to pursue a clinical position, so I focused on business courses instead. With a business background and passion for health care, my first big break came when I was working in the emergency department as an operations manager, learning how to meld the two worlds. Working in organizations with strong female role models (CEO, VP, etc.) and being close witness to the challenges and success of their positions solidified my intention to engage in executive leadership roles. Finally, being mentored both formally and informally over the course of my career by numerous individuals with diverse backgrounds continues to shape my future path.

Examples of Decisions Made

Some examples of my day-to-day decisions include human resources (e.g., hiring, discipline), procurement, contracting, capital allocation, organizational structure, service recovery, patient billing, strategic planning, and communication.

Sources of Satisfaction

A key satisfier is being trusted and respected by my current boss to produce results and engage in activities that may be seen as "breaking the rules." While we do not always agree point for point, we both have the best intentions for our patients, staff, and providers, focusing on the total person and experience. It has been my good fortune to be provided the opportunity to serve various communities, patient populations, and employee populations, and interact with a diverse group of providers.

Professional Challenges

Cultural barriers are a large challenge. Being able to transition health care as a public institution to a customer-oriented organization is a difficult task requiring focus, financing, change, and engagement. With a highly tenured staff across the organization the "we have always done it this way" organizational culture is difficult to break.

Proudest Moment as a Healthcare Manager

One of my proudest moments was seeing one of my direct reports return to college and complete a degree. The legacy that we leave as leaders is never in the information systems, bottom line savings, or process improvement; it is in the lives of those that we touch daily.

Career Goals

I hope to complete my doctorate with a focus on healthcare management and continue to grow with my present organization to larger administrative responsibilities, and ultimately be in a chief executive position at a healthcare organization.

Growth Sectors of the Industry for Healthcare Management

Ambulatory services and the outpatient environment will continue to grow at a rapid pace and will require more skilled workers. Direct-to-patient marketing, insurance regulations, and increases in technology will be the key drivers to force health care into the community and out of acute care facilities.

Professional Role Models and Mentors

My mother. She is the director of Materials Management Ancillary Services for a local Integrated Delivery Network (IDN). She has encouraged me to continue to learn and grow, not only in rhetoric, but also by completing her Master's of Healthcare Administration with me in 2008. Her poise, grace under pressure, and calm demeanor are a great influence on how I conduct myself.

Professional Mentors

The vice president of sales at a large medical supply company has been an ongoing mentor throughout my career. She has given me perspective during tough situations, provided excellent tools and feedback related to self-management and professional development, and provides an ongoing lead-by-example role model for me.

Knowledge, Skills, Abilities, and Experiences for the Next Generation of Managers

Students need both the high-level academic skills related to learning six sigma, healthcare law, contract terms, and leadership, and they also need experience at the ground level. Leadership is not given through a title, but is granted by the followers that engage with the individual, have confidence in their abilities, and respect for their knowledge. The best way to forge such relationships is to have hands-on experience in the workplace.

Advice to Students Desiring to Be Future Managers

Get out there. Volunteer, take a summer position, ask faculty how you can engage in a position while still in school. Engaging early will assist in shaping where you want to go in the future, where you don't want to go in the future, what type of organization you prefer, what type of boss who will help you to blossom, and see the breadth of positions available in healthcare management. Remember: Every day in healthcare management is an adventure.

NON-DIRECT CARE

Jerod M. Loeb, PhD

Executive Vice President for Quality Measurement and Research,
The Joint Commission

Education Completed

City University of New York, College of Staten Island, BS, Biology, 1971
State University of New York, Downstate Medical Center, PhD,
 Physiology, 1976
Harvard University, Peter Bent Brigham Hospital, Postdoctoral Fellow,
 1976–1977
Loyola University Stritch School of Medicine, Postdoctoral Fellow,
 1977–1979

How First Became Interested in Healthcare Management

I progressively gravitated toward this career from a traditional "blood-and-guts" medical school faculty position. This career gave me a chance to influence health policy at a national level.

Events That Influenced Career

Being targeted by the animal rights movement as a young faculty member, I realized I could do more as a manager, working on issues pertinent to public policy and health policy. Over time, I have assumed positions of increased responsibility as a manager. I learned early on that a good grounding in science teaches one how to think about issues in a rigorous manner—the specifics of the discipline are almost irrelevant.

Examples of Decisions Made

I have general management oversight for a division with 50 staff, divided between those who are working on a variety of health services research projects and those who develop and test performance measures. My decisions are high level, as I strongly believe in delegating the operational decision making to those best in a position to make the decisions.

Sources of Satisfaction

Working for an organization with an important mission, vision, and values is most satisfying.

Professional Challenges

The difficulty of being dependent (at least in part) on extramural grant funds is a constant challenge.

Proudest Moment as a Healthcare Manager

My proudest moment in my career was when I was promoted to executive vice president of the Joint Commission.

Career Goals

I would imagine that a CEO role is next, but the issue of my age is not a small consideration at this point in my career!

Growth Sectors of the Industry for Healthcare Management

Patient safety.

Professional Role Models and Mentors

Dennis S. O'Leary, MD, the Joint Commission's immediate past president and now president emeritus, is my most recent role model. He is a true Renaissance man. I am fortunate to have worked beside him for 14 of his 21 years here. I would also place my PhD advisor (Mario Vassalle, MD) and one of my postdoctoral advisors (Walter Randall, PhD) among key role models in my career.

Knowledge, Skills, Abilities, and Experiences for the Next Generation of Managers

Numeracy, reasoning, and oral/written skills are crucial, as is computer literacy. Specific content knowledge can always be gained later.

Advice to Students Desiring to Be Future Managers

Remember that, at its root, science is a way of thinking and not a body of facts.

DIRECT CARE

Lew Lyon, PhD

MedStar SportsHealth, Vice President, MedStar Health

Education Completed

Essex Community College, AA, Physical Education, 1973
High Point College, BS, Physical Education, 1975
Morgan State University, MS, Physical Education, Minor Emphasis
    Exercise Physiology, 1985
University of Maryland, College Park, PhD, Sports Psychology, 1995

Certification and Licensure

Basic Life Support (BLS), American Heart Association
Hypnotherapist, Hypnodyne Foundation

How First Became Interested in Healthcare Management

Human physiology and medicine always intrigued me. Unfortunately, I did not have the financial wherewithal to go to medical school. I was also blessed with the physical abilities to excel in certain sports, particularly baseball. Initially, I used the two interests to build a career foundation in physical education. As my career path matured, I was chosen by Governor Hughes to head up the Maryland Commission on Physical Fitness and Sports. As a result of that position, several years later, I was provided an opportunity to develop and supervise five sports/fitness complexes in the Gulf area for the government of Saudi Arabia. This experience provided the foundation and expertise to help create and supervise health-enhancement and sports medicine facilities for several hospitals in the Baltimore area. Several years and a PhD later, I was promoted to vice president for sports medicine of an eight-hospital healthcare facility in the Baltimore–Washington area.

Events That Influenced Career

In addition to my educational pursuits my experience in professional sports had helped to influence Governor Hughes to choose me over other qualified candidates to head up the Maryland Commission on Physical Fitness and Sports. The governor's Commission ultimately played a major role in helping to enhance my networking opportunities. Finally, the synergistic effect of an advanced degree, combined with management experience in sport/exercise science at a local and international level provided opportunities for advancement in the administrative arena of health care.

Examples of Decisions Made

Decisions I typically make during the course of a day include staff coverage for contracted events; employee issues (complaints, evaluations, policies and training); financial issues (contracts, accounts receivable and payables); and relationship building and networking.

Sources of Satisfaction

Major sources of satisfaction often revolve around the creation of a hospital program/service—from its initial inception to total fruition; the thanks from patients for helping them overcome an injury/condition; and daily interaction with a wide range of scholastic, collegiate, professional, and recreational athletes.

Professional Challenges

The rapidly changing environment in health care is a huge challenge, in particular, the increasing number of uninsured and underinsured individuals.

Proudest Moment as a Healthcare Manager

No single moment comes to mind. For me, it was the road that I traveled, not the final result that gives me a sense of satisfaction and pride. Good or bad, when I look back, every experience (in some unique way) has contributed not only to who I am, but also to what I have become.

Career Goals

Ideally, I would like to continue to teach in college and possibly contribute to a book about the problems facing healthcare delivery in this country and how the United States is poorly positioned to correct it.

Growth Sectors of the Industry for Healthcare Management

Growth sectors include the introduction of medical and/or paramedical skills for students, particularly those that address primary, secondary, and tertiary healthcare interventions. Many students who come out of college and enter the workforce with career aspirations in health care possess very few clinical skills or healthcare experiences which are considered valuable in the healthcare industry.

Professional Role Models and Mentors

Congresswoman Beverly Byron: At age 27, Congresswoman Byron encouraged the governor and the appointees to the State Commission on Fitness and Sports not to be swayed by older candidates. Conversely, she encouraged everyone to take advantage of the energy and motivation that a younger person could bring to the office. Harry Rider, president of Union Memorial Hospital: I am extremely fortunate to consider him a friend and a mentor. Our conversations were and are candid. Harry provided me living testimony that a successful leader can be very direct and demanding, all the while remaining compassionate and caring.

Knowledge, Skills, Abilities, and Experiences for the Next Generation of Managers

Day-to-day clinical skills can help get a student in the healthcare "door" and separate him or her from the rest of the other applicants. Managers, however, must possess interpersonal skills to successfully network.

Advice to Students Desiring to Be Future Managers

Network every day. Volunteer, if need be, and seek to acquire skills that a healthcare administrator would find valuable.

NON-DIRECT CARE

Natassja Manzanero

Health Insurance Specialist, Department of Health and Human Services (DHHS), Centers for Medicare and Medicaid Services (CMS)

Education Completed

Towson University, BS, Healthcare Management, 2006

Education in Progress

University of Maryland University College, Master of Science in Health-care Administration Informatics, expected date of graduation 2009

How First Became Interested in Healthcare Management

I became interested in healthcare management during college. At first I started to pursue a nursing degree, but then realized in my undergraduate studies that healthcare management is the level at which decisions can be made. I have had many leadership roles throughout school and extracurricular activities, and thought that perhaps healthcare management was a calling for me.

Events That Influenced Career

The program director of the healthcare management program at Towson University, Dr. Buchbinder, influenced my path to this position. She educated me on the existence of healthcare management and the exciting and rewarding job opportunities in the field. My mother also influenced my path to this position since she works as a business office manager at a nursing home.

Examples of Decisions Made

Currently, I am supervising our summer intern within the division. I assign her daily tasks and must make decisions on which tasks she would be able to feasibly accomplish. I was also a member of a panel which had to decide which bidder would be awarded a contract with CMS. This panel had to go through rigorous review of the materials submitted by the bidders, and ultimately had to come to a consensus. I also manage a database in which data has to be analyzed by upper management and me regularly. Being a staff-level employee, business decisions are mostly made by my direct manager, and follow a hierarchical ladder of decision making, all the way up to the secretary of health, to Congress and the White House.

Sources of Satisfaction

CMS is a great place to work. I often tell people how much I love my job because of the challenges that I face and overcome and my success leading up to my current position. I am currently on a ladder promotion scale, which means I get automatic annual raises until I reach a certain grade level. The agency is very organized and has various training opportunities to help all employees grow in their career.

Professional Challenges

The challenge that I face in my role in healthcare management is dealing with the bureaucracy that exists in the federal government structure. There is a lot of red tape when it comes to decision making so the room for creativity is very limited.

Proudest Moment as a Healthcare Manager

Being an entry-level employee, I take pride in knowing that I am trusted to take on very high-level tasks, tasks that are usually taken on by senior-level colleagues. I am honored to work in a division of attorneys and master's level and higher staff. One of my proudest moments was when I was sent an e-mail by the administrator of CMS, who was Mark McClellan at the time, and he responded "good work" on a project that I completed. My manager told me that some people who have worked for CMS for 10 years have not had a response given to them by the administrator, but I was honored to have had that opportunity during my summer internship!

Career Goals

My future career goals are to continue to move up in my career ladder and eventually become a manager. I would like to work in Washington, DC, since right now my office is in Baltimore, Maryland. I aspire to encourage more Asian Americans to work for the federal government since Asian Americans only make up 3.5% of the federal workforce. I believe in encouraging diversity in the workplace; it would be a great opportunity to see the minority population increase in this business setting.

Growth Sectors of the Industry for Healthcare Management

I believe the largest growth for jobs in the next 10 years will be in the federal workforce and in hospitals. By 2010 almost one-quarter of these employees will be eligible to retire. Therefore, I think it is important to encourage and increase the education and training opportunities for healthcare managers, who are vital employees for these agencies and institutions.

Professional Role Models and Mentors

My professional role models are my mentor and my manager. My mentor has influenced my career because she is a female manager who happens to be a minority. My boss is also a female manager, and she has encouraged me to believe that women can be incredible leaders. My current mentor is a division director in the office of information services here at CMS. She has influenced my career greatly, by letting me believe in myself as a woman, letting me know that the sky is the limit, and to reach for the stars. She is a highly intelligent woman who has many contacts throughout the agency and other agencies, and has continued to inspire me through her support and encouragement throughout the years.

Knowledge, Skills, Abilities, and Experiences for the Next Generation of Managers

Students who are interested in healthcare management must have very strong verbal and written communication skills. I cannot stress enough how much writing and communication plays an important role in obtaining leadership positions in healthcare settings. A strong background in word processing, basic computer knowledge, reading, and writing all are important abilities to have.

Advice to Students Desiring to Be Future Managers

An internship is a great place to start for someone who is interested in healthcare management to know if the field is right for them. Some people may find out that the nine-to-five setting is not right for them. Healthcare management is a very rewarding field. Not only are you making high-level decisions that help beneficiaries or patients, but you also have the opportunity to be able to see where your innate and unique skills can take you. Along with the clinical aspect of health care, the business aspect of health care is a fast-paced environment where leaders thrive.

DIRECT CARE

Karen Maust

Practice Manager, Greater Baltimore Vascular Surgery

Education

Ohio State University
University of Maryland Baltimore County
University of Maryland University College

Certification and Licensure

Certified Medical Office Manager

How First Became Interested in Healthcare Management

The opportunity fell in my lap. I was on a completely different career path, when managing a medical office was offered to me on a part-time basis. I had a real aptitude for the field, and I really enjoyed it.

Events That Influenced Career

Again, the ability to work part time while starting a family was hugely influential. Although I had management experience, I had no formal training in health care per se. However, it was a field I came to thoroughly enjoy. When I started in the field 23 years ago, it was easier to come from a different background. Today it would be nearly impossible to be in practice management, in a hospital setting, without a healthcare background.

Examples of Decisions Made

With transitioning the practice from one hospital system to another, daily decisions involve electronic medical records rollout, phone systems, medical billing software, cross training, template creation, accounts receivable conversion, and so on.

Sources of Satisfaction

I enjoy committee work because it ultimately benefits the entire organization. Also, a huge source of satisfaction is the relationship I have with my bosses. These relationships give me the freedom to be more creative, flexible, and caring with my own staff members. Also, purely from a selfish perspective, I love my office, everything from the view to my chair—perfect.

Professional Challenges

In a previous organization, it was a lack of faith in the executive leadership. The executive director did not have a clue about "clinical practice management," the Joint Commission requirements, or the basics of caring for patients. He was strictly concerned with finance and numbers, numbers, numbers. Patients seemed to be left out of the picture.

Proudest Moment as a Healthcare Manager

One of my secretaries was promoted to a practice manager position. I received a thank you note from her, which read, "I truly believe that my 'education' came from one of the best in the business. I sincerely believe your next career should be in teaching." She has gone on to excel in practice management, and I continue to keep in contact with her, and watch her successes with enthusiasm.

Career Goals

I would like to continue in practice management, finish my bachelor's degree, get my master's degree, and teach a class at a community college.

Growth Sectors of the Industry for Healthcare Management

Elder care, long-term care, skilled nursing facilities

Professional Mentors

I am in the Manager Mentoring Program, and I have been assigned a newer manager to help along the way.

Knowledge, Skills, Abilities, and Experiences for the Next Generation of Managers

A more weighted knowledge in the areas of finance, compliance, and regulations

Advice to Students Desiring to Be Future Managers

Unfortunately, it is not as much fun as it used to be. It seems we are constantly walking a tightrope with government regulations. Be prepared for finance and budgeting to be a larger part of the job than you imagined.

DIRECT CARE

Michael J. McDonnell, MBA

Chief Operating Officer, Sheltering Arms Physical Rehabilitation Centers

Education Completed

St. Bonaventure University, BA, History and Education, 1975
University of Scranton, MBA, concentration in Management, 1980

How First Became Interested in Healthcare Management

When I left the Air Force and began attending graduate school, I obtained a part-time job at Allied Services, a rehabilitation hospital in Scranton, Pennsylvania, and became hooked on rehabilitation.

Events That Influenced Career

My father was a physician and my mother was a nurse. I have a great deal of respect for what they did over the years sacrificing their time for the good of others. This was always in the back of my mind as I went through school and struggled with what I should do with my life. I enjoyed teaching, but I loved being in the hospital environment. When I got the opportunity to work in a hospital in a management capacity, I never looked back. When I served as a marketing director, I saw so many things that I thought could be operated better, so I decided that I wanted to move from marketing to operations. My current position allows me to do both since one of my areas of responsibility is the marketing department.

Examples of Decisions Made

Workforce management, approving hiring for new positions or filling vacated positions, equipment purchases, expense approvals

Sources of Satisfaction

I have a lot of freedom to plan my activities and the work I pursue. I enjoy being self-directed and having the freedom to achieve my goals. I have a very supportive board of directors that are truly interested in the welfare of our community.

Professional Challenges

Continued reduction in reimbursement from Medicare, fiscal intermediary payment denials, and RAC (recovery audit contractors) audits are all challenges I face. Also, the shortage of qualified professionals and the cost to employ them are significant organizational challenges.

Proudest Moment as a Healthcare Manager

Serving my organization as interim CEO for almost a year and improving the operating results by $1.5 million during that year.

Career Goals

Continue in my current position for the next 7 to 10 years. Significantly grow the organization during that period and improve the financial and clinical results.

Growth Sectors of the Industry for Healthcare Management

Nursing, physical therapy, and occupational therapy present opportunities for healthcare management.

Professional Role Models and Mentors

Early in my career I worked with a very bright individual who encouraged me to grow and use my skills. He taught me what it took to be successful. I have learned quiet a bit from the several CEOs I have worked for; I have learned from their different styles and gained knowledge on how things can be accomplished with different approaches.

Knowledge, Skills, Abilities, and Experiences for the Next Generation of Managers

First, they need the ability to communicate clearly. In addition, they need to listen well, and be aware of those around them who have information they need. They need to be flexible and be willing to change on a dime. They should be driven to achieve goals and understand that everything matters when it comes to quality and high levels of customer service. Health care is a dynamic business that will look very different in 10 years. They need to be change agents.

Advice to Students Desiring to Be Future Managers

They need to love helping people and the pursuit of quality health care. There are so many obstacles they will face as managers that they will need to be persistent. There are many easier places to work than in health care. If they are not willing to sacrifice and understand that their choice to work in health care means that their career is one of service 24/7, then it is not the right choice for them.

DIRECT CARE

Matt Neiswanger, MSW, LNHA

Owner and Chief Operating Officer, Neiswanger Management Services

Education Completed

West Virginia University, BSW, 1990; MSW, 1991; (1995 EdD, ABD, 1995); Masters Certificate in Gerontology, 1991

Certification and Licensure

Licensed Nursing Home Administrator, Maryland, District of Columbia, Virginia

How First Became Interested in Healthcare Management

I worked as a social worker in a nursing home prior to the Omnibus Budget Reconciliation Act (OBRA) of 1987 (this act ushered in a series of landmark nursing home reform initiatives designed to significantly improve quality of care). I didn't like the way nurses treated the elderly. I was offered an administrator-in-training (AIT) position while working as a social worker. I took the position and obtained my license.

Events That Influenced Career

As a social worker in a nursing home, I had no power to effect change to make patients' lives better. I had an elderly African American patient admitted from the hospital who had previously lived in a boarding house. She went to the hospital and then transferred to our nursing home. The only thing she had with her when she was admitted was a wig and her purse. The first thing she asked for upon settling into her room was her wig, which I handed to her. It was filthy, but it gave her comfort and dignity to wear it. She seemed content in her new room, so I went about my business for the rest of the day. Before heading home that evening, I stopped back to check on her and to say goodnight, when I found her sobbing. When I asked her what was the matter, she told me the nurse had come in, took off her wig, and threw it in the trash. I went to the nurse to ask why she did it. The nurse stated "because it was filthy." I explained to the nurse that it gave the patient a sense of comfort and dignity to have her wig, but the nurse simply did not care. I went to the director of nursing (DON), who sided with her nurse. I then went to the administrator who sided with the DON. The patient's wig was discarded, along with the patient's rights. I decided that if I were to effect change, that I needed to have power. When the AIT was offered to me, I took it.

Examples of Decisions Made

Some decisions I make on a regular basis include approving or denying salary increases, setting staffing levels, and determining capital expenditures.

Professional Challenges

Some of the challenges I face are a continually changing Medicaid reimbursement climate, dealing with diversity, and a poor quality employee pool.

Proudest Moment as a Healthcare Manager

My proudest moment was when I was told by an insider at the office of healthcare quality that the chief nurse stated that my company ran good homes. The second best moment was when we opened up the free child daycare center for my employees.

Career Goals

My goal is to buy a few more nursing homes and then to turn the company over to a competent individual to run it.

Growth Sectors of the Industry for Healthcare Management

We will see growth in long-term care and assisted living facilities.

Professional Role Models and Mentors

The preceptor for my AIT was horrible to his employees, but a wizard with finances. He taught me how to make money in a nursing home; I then took that money and took care of my employees and patients once I obtained my own facilities. I am fortunate to have two mentors currently. Harry Miller, MSW, currently serves as the president for my company. He worked as the director of social work at the Veterans Administration Hospital when I worked as an administrator of a large acquired immune deficiency syndrome (AIDS) nursing home. We both worked the systems to get the needs of the patients met, as neither of our agencies had structures and systems in place to accommodate this young population at the time. My second mentor is William Adams, who now serves as CEO for my company. He was my boss for 8 years. He was/is a master at negotiating, listening, and getting right to the bottom of a matter without emotion. I still try to learn these skills from him every day.

Knowledge, Skills, Abilities, and Experiences for the Next Generation of Managers

Managers need competence and a sense of self-assuredness. Healthcare administrators are effectively the CEOs of their own organizations and need to be able to lead. If you are not comfortable in that role, then you should not take the position. When you have 200–350 employees looking to you for direction, you need to have a vision and be able to communicate that vision to your employees. You must also be able to show them how that vision will lead to a better quality of life for both them and the patients for whom they care.

Advice to Students Desiring to Be Future Managers

The rewards—both financial and personal—are excellent, however, you had better be prepared to put your heart and soul into a facility, because that is what it takes to do it right. Being a healthcare administrator is the most rewarding career that I know of. You have immediate impact on the quality of both your patients' lives and your employees' lives. While it sounds exciting and wonderful, it takes a tremendous amount of effort, heart, and soul, but it is well worth it in the end!

NON-DIRECT CARE

Ryan Novak
Sales Consultant, Synthes

Education Completed
James Madison University, BS, Health Services Administration, 2006

How First Became Interested in Healthcare Management
I was originally a double major in business and biology. I realized that both majors were very broad and I thought healthcare management offered a way to streamline my career path.

Events That Influenced Career
Relationships with others have influenced my career. I think meeting people in different careers and maintaining a relationship with them opens a lot of doors, and then it is easy to discuss with them the positives and negatives of career choices.

Examples of Decisions Made
Most of my day is spent prioritizing and planning. I must decide what accounts are priorities and where I can grow my business. Once I identify opportunities, I must come up with a strategy.

Sources of Satisfaction
I like the job that I have because, although I am not my own boss, I do not report to an office and I do not report to a manager daily. I plan my day according to how I think it will be the most productive. I have great freedom and I am happy with the compensation and benefits. I am paid on commission, which is motivation to succeed.

Professional Challenges
The growing competitiveness in the medical device industry and increasing regulations provide challenges in my job.

Proudest Moment as a Healthcare Manager

Converting business is a proud moment in my sales career. It is exciting and rewarding to close the sale.

Career Goals

I would like to become a regional manager and ultimately a vice president within my company. I would also like to get my MBA with a focus on healthcare management.

Growth Sectors of the Industry for Healthcare Management

Medicare and Medicaid

Professional Role Models and Mentors

Most recently my boss, Michele Lozito, has been my role model. I wasn't sure what sector of health care I wanted to work in, but she showed me how rewarding a career in medical devices can be. I always perceived sales-people negatively, but it can be rewarding to positively impact patient outcomes. My job is also very competitive, and she inspired me to take ownership in my territory and use my competitive nature to make the territory succeed.

Knowledge, Skills, Abilities, and Experiences for the Next Generation of Managers

Students should have knowledge in business and sciences. It is difficult to relate to the needs of the healthcare world without knowing the sciences that create the needs. I also think that students should be flexible. The healthcare world is ever changing, and I think it is essential to be able to change with it and to continue learning. Students should try to experience the healthcare world as a business (such as insurance and consulting), and as a direct care organization (e.g., nursing home, hospital, surgery center). Experiencing these aspects will lead the student to realize what fits them best. I originally thought I wanted to work for an insurance or consulting firm, but I realized that I would rather be on the hospital side because I think it is faster paced and more demanding.

Advice to Students Desiring to Be Future Managers

Continue to learn. It is important that you continue to learn either by reading, attending courses, or furthering your education. It will be very difficult to succeed in health care by limiting yourself to what you have learned in the past. The system is changing too much for individual managers to succeed without continuing to learn more.

NON-DIRECT CARE

Ryan Papa
Pharmaceutical Representative, Pfizer Inc.

Education Completed
James Madison University, BS, Health Services Administration, 2006

How First Became Interested in Healthcare Management
While studying premed for the first two-and-a-half years of college, I learned the importance of not only understanding the science behind medicine, but also the ins and outs of the business shaping our healthcare environment. As I continued my education I became more interested in a Health Services Administration degree from JMU, enrolling in classes such as healthcare policy and politics, managed care, healthcare finance, health statistics, and hospital administration.

Events That Influenced Career
My college preparation provided a great stepping stone into the pharmaceutical industry, especially when it came time to interview for one of the most sought-after positions in all of sales. The premedical training gave me a background in anatomy and physiology, chemistry, and so on, allowing me to engage in more fluent discussions with my physicians.

The Health Services Administration degree has allowed me to understand healthcare providers' needs more clearly in addition to understanding integral pieces of my job such as insurance coverage, healthcare policy, office management, and so on. Combining this knowledge with the world-class product training and sales and business development training provided by Pfizer has allowed me to set myself apart from other representatives early in my career.

Examples of Decisions Made
- Which physicians to see, when and where to see them (e.g., office, hospital, long-term care facility)

- Scheduling meetings based on accessibility of physicians (e.g., lunch product discussions, interactive CD/DVD presentations)
- Resource allocation (e.g., budgeting, marketing materials, sample distribution)
- What information to present based on previous interactions and discussions

Sources of Satisfaction

The most satisfaction I receive is from patient testimonials. To have a patient break down and cry about how a particular medicine has changed their life after so many years of pain and distress is truly moving. Another source of satisfaction is the ability to engage with one of the most respected professions in the world on a daily basis. Providing yourself as a valuable resource and being able to answer specific questions for these extensively educated physicians is quite rewarding. The flexibility and ever-changing environment of my job is another large factor influencing my satisfaction. Every day is different and new challenges arise multiple times throughout the day. The satisfaction comes into play when you are able to adjust to these challenges regularly and operate your business to produce the greatest possible outcomes.

Professional Challenges

The perception of the pharmaceutical industry is a challenge I face from both physicians and patients. In order to combat these challenges, I make sure to provide myself as a resource as opposed to a salesman. Providing patient education tools, drug samples, and making my job relevant to each individual's practice are all ways to fight the common challenge of perception. Another challenge is making sure the drug is accessible for all patients. This requires a strong knowledge of managed care, Medicare, Medicaid, formulary status, and so on. The ever-changing healthcare environment makes staying current on this information yet another challenge. One last challenge is getting time with physicians to discuss information. It is important to understand the physician's main priority (the patient) and work with the physician to develop a convenient time/method to share/discuss information.

Proudest Moment as a Healthcare Manager

Receiving an offer from the top company in my industry straight out of college with no sales experience was a huge honor and a very proud moment in my career. As my career has progressed the recognition from my district manager and regional manager in regard to my clinical knowledge/business relationships/acumen/sales goals and so on has given me a lot of pride in what I do and how I conduct myself on a daily basis. Working for such a large company, it can be easy to get caught in the shuffle, but when your mentors and leadership team take notice of you early in your career, it provides a lot of motivation for continued growth and development.

Career Goals

My first goal is to be promoted into a specialty representative position dealing with hospitals and specialists exclusively. Following that, I would like to continue to increase my roles and responsibilities and move into a leadership/management position at the district, regional, and/or national levels.

Growth Sectors of the Industry for Healthcare Management

- Hospital Administration: Unfortunately there will always be sick/injured people
- Healthcare Consulting: Cost saving is key
- Healthcare Information Technology: The industry is moving to a paperless system

Professional Role Models and Mentors

My father has always been a professional role model of mine based on his professional growth and development over the years. His drive, determination, attention to detail, and organizational skills have all served as great examples to me both personally and professionally. He climbed the ranks in the Navy as a helicopter pilot and after retiring, he embarked on a new challenge in defense contracting, quickly establishing himself as the VP of the company. Directly related to my position, I have had multiple role models and mentors, including my district manager, Jay Alexander, who established himself as a strong leader very early in his career, again exemplifying the ideal traits to grow and have continued success within the pharmaceutical industry. My first direct counterpart, Gail Gravell, who has over a decade within the pharmaceutical industry, also provided a lot of support and guidance early in my career. Her relationship building and her availability as a resource to the office have been two areas I have tried to mirror in my career.

Knowledge, Skills, Abilities, and Experiences for the Next Generation of Managers

Since health care is so multifaceted, it is important that future leaders in health care be well-rounded and exposed to all areas of health care. This will allow future managers to be a more valuable resource to their organization. Through interacting with all levels of health care (e.g., physicians, suppliers, other health organizations, human resources, finance, managed care, etc.) future managers will need to understand the needs and perspectives of those working within the system, in addition to those individuals working directly within a healthcare organization.

Advice to Students Desiring to Be Future Managers

Find out what motivates you and pursue it with drive and passion. As with anything else in life you will get out what you put in. If you lose this drive and passion, there are numerous settings within health care to explore and the characteristics and knowledge most healthcare managers possess can be utilized positively across many of these healthcare arenas.

DIRECT CARE

Reena Patel

Consultant, Virginia Department of Health, Division of Immunization

Education Completed

James Madison University, BS, Health Services Administration and
Public Health, 2007

Education in Progress

Planning to pursue an MPH at Virginia Commonwealth University

How First Became Interested in Healthcare Management

I became interested in healthcare management because I knew it would
give me a variety of options as far as employment as well as a balance
between my areas of interest—business and health.

Events That Influenced Career

I always wanted to be involved in health care in one way or another. I
completed an internship with my current employer while completing my
BS degree, which led to my current position.

Examples of Decisions Made

I'm involved in the statewide immunization registry project. We are still in
our implementation phase, and it requires a lot of decisions on business
planning, creating regulations, budgeting, development and implementation of training plans, and progress reporting, among others.

Professional Challenges

Finding opportunity for professional growth and career advancement are
challenges I face. Compensation and benefits create another challenge
when working at the state level.

Proudest Moment as a Healthcare Manager

When my manager retired, I was able to lead the registry project and show that I am qualified for a management position. This was a proud moment for me.

Career Goals

I would like to go back to school and pursue a career in a field that allows me to interact with other direct care providers, such as nurses.

Growth Sectors of the Industry for Healthcare Management

There is a lot of opportunity in the information technology sector of health care.

Professional Role Models and Mentors

My previous boss, Archer Redmond, was a great influence on me. She taught me a large portion of what I know today. She gave me the firsthand work experience that I needed that cannot be taught in a classroom. She was previously the business/project manager for the immunization registry.

Knowledge, Skills, Abilities, and Experiences for the Next Generation of Managers

Students should be taught more skills on the technical side of health care.

Advice to Students Desiring to Be Future Managers

Take the opportunity to get as much experience in the field as possible before making career choices.

NON-DIRECT CARE

Justine Powell

Sales Administration Analyst, CIGNA HealthCare

Education Completed

James Madison University, BS, Health Services Administration, 2006

Certification or Licensure

Health Insurance License; pursuing Certified Employee Benefits Specialist (CEBS)

How First Became Interested in Healthcare Management

I was initially interested in being a dietitian. A year and a half into my studies at JMU as a Dietetics major, I determined that the clinical side of health care was not for me. I had always had an interest in business and health care, so it seemed like the Health Services Administration major was a perfect fit.

Events That Influenced Career

Thus far in my career, I would say that having a mentor at my current employer has helped me to succeed and excel in my position, encouraged me to think about what positions I may want in the future, and in general, has helped to jump-start my career at this, my first professional employment experience.

Examples of Decisions Made

I decide whether to pursue quoting on a prospect or not, based on claims experience, group characteristics, and other competitive reasons. Also, in conjunction with the salesperson, I help to formulate a strategy for how we can win our prospective client's business.

Sources of Satisfaction

Within my organization, there are unlimited opportunities to learn, grow, and explore other positions. My colleagues are very willing to share their knowledge and experience in order to help me grow. I enjoy building relationships with both internal and external partners. It is rewarding to be considered a trusted partner by both CIGNA employees and my external contacts.

Professional Challenges

This sales cycle has been particularly challenging. As a result of the economic climate and competition, we have faced significant challenges in trying to make sales. This can be especially frustrating, but it is important to persevere.

Proudest Moment as a Healthcare Manager

My proudest moment thus far has been receiving a promotion 10 months into my first position, which often takes others 3 to 5 years to obtain. I believe that my bachelor's degree in Health Services Administration, my desire to succeed, and the positive reinforcement from my mentor all led to my promotion.

Career Goals

In the future, I hope to move into a client management position in which I would work with clients to develop their health benefits packages while keeping in mind their financial needs and long-term goals.

Growth Sectors of the Industry for Healthcare Management

As the baby boomers continue to get older, I believe that healthcare services for the over 65 population will be an area of significant growth.

Professional Role Models and Mentors

My father has been a professional role model in my career. About 10 years ago, he completed the certification he needed to work in a field that he loves. He encouraged me to think about what interests me and to pursue that as a career. As a result, I pursued my interests in health care and business, and I am very happy with the field that I have chosen. I believe that being truly interested in your field of work is a major component of having a successful career.

I have a mentor that works with me now. His title is new business manager/sales executive, and he is the salesperson I support. He has challenged me to always strive for excellence in what I am doing, which has created a level of accountability between us. Once I started in my position, he immediately saw the value in sharing his knowledge with me so that we could become a strong team. He often quizzes me on topics to make sure that I am well versed on our company's underwriting methodologies and competitive differentiators. As a result of all the time that he has taken to "develop" me, I feel that my career is on the fast track at CIGNA.

Knowledge, Skills, Abilities, and Experiences for the Next Generation of Managers

Have an internship experience. The internship that I completed as a part of my bachelor's degree was invaluable in helping me to determine what I wanted to do and provided me with experience that was important for getting my first job. Also, be open to change. The healthcare field will likely change significantly over the next 10 to 20 years, and the only way to be successful during a time of such change is to keep an open mind.

Advice to Students Desiring to Be Future Managers

Find someone in your organization that you admire and respect, and ask that person if they would be willing to be a mentor for you. It is invaluable to have a trusted partner within your organization to whom you can ask questions and from whom you can learn.

DIRECT CARE

Jeff Richardson, MBA, LCSW-C
Executive Director, Mosaic Community Services

Education Completed

Towson University, BS, Psychology Clinical Concentration, 1986
University of Maryland School of Social Work, MSW, concentration in
   Community Organizing and Clinical Administration, 1991
Loyola College Maryland, MBA, 2000

How First Became Interested in Healthcare Management

As a practitioner, I became aware that I might be able to have a greater
impact on those who I served as a healthcare manager.

Events That Influenced Career

I was able to play a role in a series of organizational changes such as merg-
ers and reorganizations, combined with a degree of random good luck.

Professional Challenges

I face constant funding challenges, workforce challenges, and work stress.

Proudest Moment as a Healthcare Manager

I have been lucky to have many. Most come from people we have been able
to help.

Career Goals

Keep growing and developing the organization. Having opportunities to
develop and teach others.

Growth Sectors of the Industry for Healthcare Management

You can't go wrong with any health sector serving seniors.

Professional Role Models and Mentors

I have been fortunate to have some very talented supervisors and board presidents. The most important message they conveyed was the enormous value of the work in health care we provide.

Knowledge, Skills, Abilities, and Experiences for the Next Generation of Managers

You must have solid business training. Many clinicians are promoted into leadership in health care without financial, business, and managerial skills.

Advice to Students Desiring to Be Future Managers

Be willing to try different opportunities. I am very grateful for my career in healthcare management and hope others will pursue this tremendously gratifying experience!

NON-DIRECT CARE

Andrea Saevoon

Component Administrator, American Physical Therapy Association (APTA)

Education Completed

James Madison University, BS, Health Services Administration, 2007

How First Became Interested in Healthcare Management

I first became interested in healthcare management in college and decided to pursue it as my major. I thought it was a great combination of skills: health, business, communication, and writing, to name but a few. It is also a challenging and a constantly developing discipline, which keeps it interesting for me.

Events That Influenced Career

My education at JMU, especially in the Health Services Administration program, is the most influential part of my experience and path to my current position. I also think that my experience at Inova Health System during my internship and experience in consulting also impacted my decision and path to my current position at APTA.

Examples of Decisions Made

Some examples of decisions I make on a day-to-day basis include how to best communicate with members and the board of directors, how to go about planning meetings, and how materials should be organized and presented.

Sources of Satisfaction

My job is satisfying because I have great relationships with all the APTA staff. I know that there are helpful and supportive coworkers around me and this really makes it easy to come to work every day. I also love that I get to interact with members on a daily basis and can help them directly. I know my work is appreciated, and I love that feeling.

Professional Challenges

I haven't faced any challenges yet, but I know in the future balancing a family and a career will be hard. It is not directly related to healthcare management, but it is an issue some women face.

Proudest Moment as a Healthcare Manager

My proudest moment as a healthcare manager is directly helping other people.

Career Goals

I'm not quite sure. Perhaps I will pursue an advanced degree.

Growth Sectors of the Industry for Healthcare Management

Geriatrics is one of the biggest growth sectors for healthcare management.

Professional Role Models and Mentors

My supervisor and coworkers at Inova Health System, BearingPoint, and APTA have all encouraged me to pursue what I love to do.

Knowledge, Skills, Abilities, and Experiences for the Next Generation of Managers

The next generation of managers will need flexibility, passion, communication skills, and organization skills.

Advice to Students Desiring to Be Future Managers

Healthcare management is interesting and rewarding.

NON-DIRECT CARE

Jennifer R. Shapiro, MPH

Director, Division of Benefit Purchasing and Monitoring,
Centers for Medicare and Medicaid Services (Medicare Drug
Benefit and C&D Data Group)

Education Completed

Oberlin College, BA, East Asian Studies, 1995
Johns Hopkins University, School of Public Health, MPH, 2001

How First Became Interested in Healthcare Management

Actually, I fell into healthcare management. Instead of seeking a specific job that interested me because of the topic, I sought a job that used skills that I loved to employ. I wanted to find something where I would interact with others and use hardcore analytic, writing, and communication skills. Nearing college graduation I decided that "consulting" would employ all of those skills so I applied to a variety of consulting firms. I ended up accepting a job with The Lewin Group, which just happened to have a focus on health care. I ended up loving it.

Events That Influenced Career

Top-notch mentors. I have been very fortunate to have brilliant mentors in my career.

Examples of Decisions Made

Some of my day-to-day decisions include how to staff projects, structure and content of leadership briefing papers, prioritizing work assignments from staff (since we always have more to do than we can handle), what types of compliance actions to implement when a breach has occurred among one of the Part D sponsors, which issues need to be elevated to leadership, and selection of analytical methods used for specific projects.

Sources of Satisfaction

I love the intensity of my work. It never slows down, is never boring, and new challenges arise almost daily. I also feel that my work is important. Millions of Medicare beneficiaries are affected by my day-to-day activities, even though it's sometimes easy to forget that. Congress, Wall Street, and many others also scrutinize my organization's activities. I am also fortunate to work with people who are truly the best in government. My staff are exceptionally talented and I give them the freedom and room to excel and shine. At the same time, I enjoy leading the group and providing support whenever it is required.

Professional Challenges

Challenges in my role include hiring freezes and limited resources. Also, communication can be a challenge in a large bureaucratic environment. However, the leadership team is striving every day to improve communication and coordination across boundaries.

Career Goals

I will probably stay with the federal government. Eventually I would hope to move higher into the federal leadership ranks.

Knowledge, Skills, Abilities, and Experiences for the Next Generation of Managers

Writing skills!

Advice to Students Desiring to Be Future Managers

Know thyself. That is, be honest and critical about your strongest skills and what you really enjoy doing on a day-to-day basis. Then match those skills to the best job for you.

NON-DIRECT CARE

Sunil K. Sinha, MD, MBA, FACHE

Federal Field Medical Policy Director, Pfizer Inc.

Education Completed

Bangalore University, India, MBBS, 1989
Southern Illinois University, MBA, 1998

How First Became Interested in Healthcare Management

As an associate chief resident, I became involved in administration and decided to pursue an MBA to get a better understanding of the administration and business aspect of medicine.

Events That Influenced Career

I've had many opportunities which have taken me to the next phase of my career. My associate chief resident experience got me interested in pursuing the business side of medicine. My MBA landed me my first operations job, without any "real experience." The added responsibility of performance improvement in my job at Baltimore piqued my interest in performance and quality improvement work. That work—my performance and quality improvement experience—made me qualified for my job at CMS (Medicare). I happened to be at CMS at the time the Part D drug benefit was being rolled out, and I became a senior medical officer for the program. All of the above collective experience with operations, quality and performance improvement, and work experience for the federal government and Medicare landed me my present job at Pfizer.

Examples of Decisions Made

I manage relationships with numerous national and regional healthcare entities and have to make decisions on how to engage with them on certain activities, and if they are beneficial or not for my company.

Sources of Satisfaction

I have had the good fortune to have had excellent bosses who have been supportive, and provided guidance without being a barrier, to do things I feel have helped the organizations I have served, and in turn helped me in my own career growth.

Professional Challenges

As with all of health care, my biggest challenge is not being able to make sustainable and significant improvements in the quality and performance of our health systems.

Proudest Moment as a Healthcare Manager

I am most proud of my ongoing work at the Department of Veterans Affairs, helping our veterans.

Career Goals

I keep looking for opportunities to make a difference.

Growth Sectors of the Industry for Healthcare Management

The next big waves are "creative" healthcare financing and the use of information technology.

Professional Role Models and Mentors

I've learned something from each of my supervisors in terms of the importance of good work ethics, focus and preparation for the job, and treating people with respect.

Knowledge, Skills, Abilities, and Experiences for the Next Generation of Managers

Good work ethics, focus and preparation for the job, and treating people with respect . . . these qualities are timeless.

Advice to Students Desiring to Be Future Managers

In the first few years, try to gain a variety of experiences (HR, IT, clinical, administration, etc) through jobs and volunteerism, which will help you see medicine and health care from different perspectives, and help you decide where you may "best fit."

NON-DIRECT CARE

Justin E. Skinner, MFA, MBA

Manager of Market Planning and Analysis, CareFirst BlueCross BlueShield

Education Completed

California State University Sacramento, BA, 1995
Towson University, MFA, Theatre, 1999
Loyola College of Maryland, MBA, Business, 2005

How First Became Interested in Healthcare Management

I pursued an MBA to get a wider knowledge base of business fundamentals—after I completed the degree, I wanted to put what I had learned into practice more than I would have been able to at the Children's Museum. I decided to try to get a job in the largest industry in the nation, which is healthcare, because I figured that would give me good exposure to a wide range of business problems in a dynamic and changing environment.

Events That Influenced Career

Primarily my MBA degree influenced my career. But if I look way back, I did a consultant project in market research which required heavy use of Microsoft Excel. I honestly believe that a good chunk of my success stems from my extensive knowledge of Excel. It seems that there is a lot of mystery around manipulating data and creating pretty charts and graphs.

Examples of Decisions Made

Part of my job is to communicate marketplace changes on a regular basis. Decisions need to be made about what information is relevant for our senior management. Another example is creating a business plan. There are always more things our department wants to get done in a year than money and/or time allows. Decisions need to be made as to what items take priority.

Professional Challenges

Currently I have a relatively new employee that is not succeeding as well as I would like. Trying to get her to create higher quality work is a major challenge. Also, our organization has a new CEO who has different expectations from the previous CEO. Trying to understand and be proactive to his needs is challenging because I don't have an intuitive feel for what data or information he may want.

Proudest Moment as a Healthcare Manager

My proudest moment in my career was being promoted to manager within a year of entering a completely new field.

Career Goals

My goal is to be a leader, in practice and title, of an organization. It doesn't necessarily have to be the one I am in now, nor does it have to be in health care.

Growth Sectors of the Industry for Healthcare Management

The healthcare industry is far behind other industries in information technology (IT) development and management and needs to catch up to cut costs and increase quality.

Knowledge, Skills, Abilities, and Experiences for the Next Generation of Managers

The next generation will need IT skills and business skills.

Advice to Students Desiring to Be Future Managers

It's a big industry with a lot of opportunity. The most important thing is to spend the time to try to find exactly what you want to do. Find several internships and/or entry-level jobs at different organizations. This will give you a good perspective of the entire industry and not just one function. My background is more from a business perspective. The healthcare industry is a very challenging business model. This has made it very exciting to me.

DIRECT CARE

Wes Street, NHA
Executive Director, Sunrise Senior Living

Education Completed
Salisbury University, BS, Business Administration, 1991

How First Became Interested in Healthcare Management
I became interested as a senior in high school when my father became ill. I did some research in college, and I loved history. This field gave me a chance to give back to the people who made our country what it is today. It was the least I felt I could do.

Events That Influenced Career
The passing of my father was the primary event that led me to this position. As my career went along, the stories of residents that just simply wanted to talk kept me involved. The intrinsic rewards I receive by spending time with the resident and seeing a smile make it all worthwhile.

Examples of Decisions Made
The decisions made on a day-to-day basis are more for the future. Examples are new products or services, budget parameters, market strategies, and what is best for the people we care for at the end of the day.

Professional Challenges
Challenges I face include the day-to-day changes in regulations, the housing market, and economy; issues of reimbursement in health care; and the work ethic of the generation entering the work force.

Proudest Moment as a Healthcare Manager
My proudest moment was writing a letter to Hall-of-Famer Brooks Robinson for a resident who knew Mr. Robinson very well. Mr. Robinson called

me a few days later, and wanted to visit the resident. As he arrived he quickly found out that he knew several other residents living with us at the time. The residents and Brooks Robinson spent an entire afternoon sharing stories of the past. They were all so happy to have spent the time together, and just watching brought tears to my eyes.

Career Goals

I aspire to work with a professional baseball organization.

Growth Sectors of the Industry for Healthcare Management

Long-term care

Knowledge, Skills, Abilities, and Experiences for the Next Generation of Managers

They must have compassion and can never become desensitized to their feelings.

Advice to Students Desiring to Be Future Managers

Treat people as you would like to be treated. Do not jump into the first thing that comes your way. Do your homework on a company. It is a rewarding experience, but you must have a life outside of work.

NON-DIRECT CARE

Richard J. Stull, FACHE
Executive Director, IPC The Hospitalist Company

Education Completed

Central Methodist University, BS, Business Administration, 1970

Certification or Licensure

Certificate in Hospital Administration, Charlotte Memorial Hospital, 1972
Fellow, American College of Healthcare Executives (FACHE)

How First Became Interested in Healthcare Management

I was born into it! My father was the administrator of Phoenixville Hospital where I was born and he signed my birth certificate. Also, after graduating from college he convinced me that it was an excellent and rewarding industry for a career.

Events That Influenced Career

After managing the North Broward Hospital District in Florida for over 20 years (a public system with the board appointed by the governor), then managing Pediatrix and completing its Initial Public Offering (IPO), I took 5 years off. After moving to Colorado for a change of environment, I wanted to get back into the healthcare world but with something that was new and different, and that could make a positive change in our industry. The hospitalist specialty of medicine was the answer.

Examples of Decisions Made

I make strategic decisions on growth, expansion into other facilities, growth within existing facilities, and recruitment.

Sources of Satisfaction

My market is one market within the company. I have the freedom to plan and grow the business without limitations. This happens either by acquiring new hospitalist groups, getting hospital contracts, hiring more doctors to serve the existing market, and employing the best physicians who will become a part of the team at each hospital.

Professional Challenges

Herding the cats—managing our doctors—is a challenge. Also, being non-clinical in a clinical environment requires a delicate balance in managing the doctors to perform at their best. One of the biggest challenges is getting the doctors to understand the concept of being an employee or part of something bigger.

Proudest Moment as a Healthcare Manager

Turning around the financially troubled North Broward Hospital District in 1 year and then having the ability to provide more and better healthcare services to our indigent population was a proud moment for me. Also, receiving my Fellowship from ACHE was a very proud moment.

Career Goals

Continue to work with IPC to make it the best hospitalist company that truly impacts the quality and cost of health care in a positive manner. Continue to participate in the Colorado Association of Healthcare Executives and hopefully provide an example for our industry's younger managers.

Growth Sectors of the Industry for Healthcare Management

This is a very difficult question but the fact remains that there are always going to be jobs for dedicated, hard-working individuals. Part of the problem, though, is that you can teach management but you can't teach converting the education into successful management. That only comes with experience.

Professional Role Models and Mentors

There is no doubt that my father was always my role model. While struggling in college (too much playing) I always knew I could be successful because of the support that I received from my father and all the things that I learned through osmosis by being around him. It is important to note that many individuals who served as a role model did so by their negative performance or actions—I learned what not to do. My mentor now is myself: to continue to work, grow, and give to this industry.

Knowledge, Skills, Abilities, and Experiences for the Next Generation of Managers

The knowledge is the basic understanding of the complexities of this industry and particularly the sector of their interest. The abilities are to be very ethical, honest, and the ability to be willing to make a mistake and learn from it—in other words, make a decision.

Advice to Students Desiring to Be Future Managers

Do it and you will never regret it!

Final Comment

I think the industry has lost much of the camaraderie that has existed in the past, possibly due to the stress of competition. Also, many of our senior people seem to get to a level where they feel they don't need to participate in many of the state association education sessions where the younger folks attend and are looking for mentors. This would be a big help to future healthcare managers.

NON-DIRECT CARE

Jeanine Tyler

Market Manager, Apria Healthcare

Education Completed

Towson University, BS, Healthcare Management, 2003

How First Became Interested in Healthcare Management

I had always been interested in the healthcare industry, but didn't necessarily want to follow a clinical path. I also have an interest in business; therefore, healthcare management was a natural fit. Educating health professionals on products and services and managing sales representatives is an extremely rewarding field with many natural benefits to all involved.

Events That Influenced Career

A series of personal health issues and a chronic illness sparked my interest in the healthcare field. Having leaders within the company believing in my abilities and giving me the confidence that I am capable of running my own market has been extremely influential. That type of belief is powerful in developing a young professional, along with support and continuous encouragement.

Examples of Decisions Made

My decisions usually involve operational decisions that support smart business planning and could potentially support or affect the profit-and-loss statement.

Sources of Satisfaction

I am very pleased with my ability to grow a historically difficult market 23% by revenue versus the 10% typically achieved under previous leadership. The ability to mentor, develop, and manage sales representatives and watch them grow personally and professionally gives me great satisfaction.

Professional Challenges

Communication and getting everyone on the same page in a company that is segmented between sales and operations is a professional challenge. A task as simple as communication can be a major obstacle in organizations. Also, keeping a sales representative highly motivated and stretching them to the fullest of their ability on a daily basis is a focus area for managers.

Trouble shooting operational issues and knowing what makes sense and when to turn down business is also another challenge. In order to gain market share you must stay competitive, now more than ever. With reimbursement cuts with Medicare and various insurances, we need to get paid and allow the profit-and-loss statement to stay ahead. This drives strategic business decision making and going after business to enable the organization to survive.

Proudest Moment as a Healthcare Manager

My proudest moment was when I was selected as Market Manager of the Year in 2007, which was the first year I managed a historically difficult market.

Career Goals

My goal is to continue to grow within the current company of employment. I hope to be offered the next step as a regional vice president (RVP) of sales.

Growth Sectors of the Industry for Healthcare Management

With the aging of the baby boomer generation, anything with geriatrics will be a growth area.

Professional Mentors

My mentor is my boss, who is the RVP. He identified my ability before I did. He keeps me motivated.

Knowledge, Skills, Abilities, and Experiences for the Next Generation of Managers

Organization-specific knowledge can be learned at the company a student chooses to pursue. But, experience is priceless and can only be acquired by networking, doing internships, and creating a name for yourself. Communication, follow-up skills, positive personality, confidence, and self-awareness are the biggest skills and abilities needed for healthcare management.

Advice to Students Desiring to Be Future Managers

It takes a certain person who has to be able to problem-solve, multitask, delegate, and communicate. Remember, in the end, it is about the patient, who should never be lost in the shuffle. If you have a passion with your chosen field, it isn't viewed as work, it is viewed as making a difference on a daily basis.

DIRECT CARE

Jennifer Villani, MPH

Program Analyst, National Institute of General Medical Sciences (NIGMS)

Education Completed

James Madison University, BS, Health Services Administration, 2004
George Washington University, School of Public Health and Health
    Services, MPH, Epidemiology, 2005

Education in Progress

University of Maryland, College Park, PhD, Health Services
    Administration

How First Became Interested in Healthcare Management

My interest in healthcare management started when I interned at a local
health department. I was given the assignment of creating a marketing tool
for the entire agency. I interviewed each of the nine department chiefs to
find out the essence of their work. I was impressed with their commitment
to public health. Even though they didn't do any of the frontline work,
they still had the same motivation for helping individuals get access to
affordable health care. From that point forward, I always wanted to be a
public servant. When National Institutes of Health (NIH) made me an
offer, I jumped on it. I couldn't pass up the opportunity to work for the
nation's premier medical research agency.

Events That Influenced Career

My career is still very young. The biggest event that influenced my path
was going to graduate school straight out of college. I knew I wanted a
degree in Public Health so I pursued it immediately. After that, I easily
found a job at the National Association of County and City Health Officials (NACCHO). I loved working there and representing the interests of
local public health agencies. However, after only a short while, the NIH
came calling.

Examples of Decisions Made

Hiring and managing contractors to carry out various tasks, evaluating the progress of research programs, and analyzing data about effects of program policies are typical decision-making activities in my position.

Sources of Satisfaction

My job satisfaction stems from my boss giving me the freedom to be as ambitious as I am. I work hard and I am recognized for my efforts. I have great colleagues and a very supportive organizational climate. Plus I am able to walk to work. What's not to like?

Professional Challenges

My challenges are not specific to healthcare management. No matter where you work, you will have to deal occasionally with a difficult coworker, and you will always have multiple demands competing for your time and attention.

Proudest Moment as a Healthcare Manager

Any project that I have led from start to completion is a source of pride for me.

Career Goals

After I receive my PhD, I plan to continue my career in the government at NIH, the Health Resources and Services Administration (HRSA), or the Agency for Healthcare Research and Quality (AHRQ) in more of a managerial role overseeing an office whose focus is improving the nation's healthcare system in some way, shape, or form.

Growth Sectors of the Industry for Healthcare Management

I believe there will be a growing need for healthcare managers dealing with health information technology (e.g., electronic medical records), or in government if the nation embraces universal health care.

Professional Role Models and Mentors

John Whitmarsh, PhD, special assistant to the NIGMS director is my mentor. He recruited me to NIH and has taught me a number of important life lessons that have guided my career path.

Knowledge, Skills, Abilities, and Experiences for the Next Generation of Managers

Appreciation of multiculturalism, ability to articulate oneself via written and oral communication, and the ability to demonstrate analytical skills will be necessary for the next generation of managers.

Advice to Students Desiring to Be Future Managers

Find a mentor who genuinely cares about your career advancement and is willing to take time out of his or her schedule to give you advice on how to achieve your goals. Then, when you have succeeded, provide the same support to the next generation of healthcare managers.

NON-DIRECT CARE

Jason Vollmer

Northeast Regional Accounts Manager, Maxim Staffing Solutions

Education Completed

Towson University, BS, Healthcare Management, 2001

How First Became Interested in Healthcare Management

I began as a premed major and after 2 years, I realized that hands-on patient care was not for me. I still wanted to stay in the healthcare profession, so I decided to change majors to a study that involved more of the management aspect of health care. I sought out a program and the Healthcare Management (HCMN) program that Towson University offered caught my eye. It incorporated the healthcare-related courses that I completed, as well as a minor in Business Administration.

Events That Influenced Career

Going into college, if someone was to ask me if I wanted a career in sales, I probably would not have considered it. However, Towson's HCMN program offered a large selection and variety of internship opportunities and settings from which I could choose. I researched the companies so as to gain the most of the experience. I chose to interview with Maxim Healthcare Services for my internship and was immediately intrigued with their culture, people, and earning potential.

At this time, I learned the reality of a sales profession and it changed my perception of that career track. I have always been personable, competitive, and hard working, which fits a profession in sales very well. There are many factors in my life that shaped me as an individual; however, the internship program required in the HCMN major is what solidified my decision to pursue this career path. Upon completion of my internship, I was offered a position within Maxim and eagerly accepted.

Examples of Decisions Made

I have been with Maxim Healthcare Services for over 7 years and have been in different positions, which involve different levels of decisions. As a recruiter, an entry-level position, I had the ability to hire healthcare professionals for assignments within the medical industry. Positions varied from one-on-one nursing care in the home to highly skilled medical positions in a hospital. Taking the time to screen and make a final call on hiring someone to send them to an assignment is extremely important, especially when the reputation of our company is behind every hour worked by our staff.

As a branch manager, there are a lot of short-term and long-term decisions that need to be made. I wore many hats and there was a lot of planning and management involved. A branch manager runs an office from the top to bottom. When I was the manager of our Silver Spring Staffing office, I made the business decision to make the focus of the office hospital staffing. I had to strategize and direct my office to do the appropriate recruiting of healthcare personnel with hospital experience, as well as form a sales strategy to gain hospitals as clients. By focusing my vision, I was able to increase the business within the hospital industry in the Washington metropolitan region by over 500% over a 2-year period, and followed that by consistent double-digit growth. Another important decision I had to make was the team I created in the office. Without the right people the office would not have been successful. Even now as a district manager, it is important to understand that the people you work with are your most important asset. The individuals that we bring into our doors have to have that same desire to succeed, buy into our culture, and have the enthusiasm to work hard.

Sources of Satisfaction

Weekly, I walk into an office and meet with an entire team to offer resources to aid them in becoming successful and foster their personal and professional growth. It is extremely satisfying to see those individuals promoted and take that office to another level of success. Throughout the week, I will have one-on-one conversations with the team in that branch to see where they are in their development. I bring in a more global view of the company and industry and bring more of a sense of camaraderie by bringing the offices together. Watching others grow and succeed is extremely gratifying. It is also extremely satisfying to see the business plan for new markets come to life. There is a lot that goes into the planning of an office opening. Once the new office opens and starts making profits, I know that I am playing a large part in the growth of our organization.

Professional Challenges

A large part of my success and the success of the company revolves around the people with whom I work. The largest challenge is identifying an individual that is loyal, willing to put in the extra hours, and has a goal to lead others. The secondary challenge definitely falls behind the healthcare professional shortage!

Proudest Moment as a Healthcare Manager

The proudest moment was when I promoted my first recruiter to the account manager role. I worked closely with this individual and seeing him develop and become successful within the company was satisfying. Seeing the growth and the differences you make in a career is very rewarding.

Career Goals

My professional goals are constantly changing as my career evolves. As a district manager, the most consistent goal is to continually grow the team around me and have all of them hit their personal and professional goals. As a leader, I see their success as my own. Also, their success will lead to the ultimate goal of having our company be the number one healthcare staffing company. More importantly, my career goals give me the ability to achieve personal goals: financial independence and the ability to have a strong work/life balance.

Growth Sectors of the Industry for Healthcare Management

Health care is an industry that will survive many challenges. It will continue to evolve and grow throughout economic struggles due to the fact that it is a constantly needed product. Healthcare management encompasses many different types of positions and an individual really has a lot of flexibility. Government-funded health programs are consistently expanding, hospitals are consistently expanding their services and size, and many private companies that service facilities are on the rise.

Professional Role Models and Mentors

It is really difficult to identify one individual. Our company has a very strong culture of sharing opinions and an environment where you can bounce ideas and challenges off one another. Most of these individuals are currently at the executive level. This open communication with colleagues at various stages of tenure has allowed me to grow as a professional leader and manager.

Knowledge, Skills, Abilities, and Experiences for the Next Generation of Managers

Experience, attitude, personality, and ethics are what next-generation managers need to excel as a professional and gain a competitive edge. They also need to be able to take constructive criticism and, more importantly, learn from it. One particular attribute that is necessary to succeed is the need to go above and beyond the "call of duty." I did not get in my position by working by the time clock, but instead worked until the job was done. New graduates are often shocked at our expectations, including the long work hours and high levels of responsibility they will have. Personality plays a big part in an interview, and we look for a correlation between experiences that people have and their open personality. Anyone who has been in the service industry, taken part in extracurricular activities, played sports, or has been part of a social club tends to do well in our company.

Advice to Students Desiring to Be Future Managers

There are unlimited options out there. It is a great major to pursue. Make sure you are willing to work hard and be persistent. To be a good manager you must lead by example; to be a great manager you must be willing to be driven by the success of others.

NON-DIRECT CARE

Tanisha Woodard

Analyst, Mercer Health and Benefits

Education Completed

James Madison University, BS, Health Services Administration, 2005

Education in Progress

George Washington University, Master of Public Health and Health
  Policy, expected date of completion, December 2010

Certification or Licensure

Life and Health Insurance License

How First Became Interested in Healthcare Management

My father recommended I pursue this degree after discussing my interests
with a coworker. I was particularly interested in managing others and
demonstrating leadership while keeping my interest in health care.

Events That Influenced Career

Several of my family members are involved in consulting and I found it a
good first career to become exposed to many different types of people and
blossom my career quickly.

Examples of Decisions Made

Some of the decisions I make on a daily basis include project delegation to
analysts who support me on my accounts, assisting clients with decisions
surrounding managing healthcare costs, choosing appropriate vendors and
plans, and creating marketing strategies.

Sources of Satisfaction

My job is satisfying because it is challenging, I work with great people, and I am recognized consistently for a job well-done.

Professional Challenges

The biggest challenge I face currently is how to help clients provide satisfactory benefit plans to their employees while keeping costs reasonable given the state of the economy.

Proudest Moment as a Healthcare Manager

My proudest moment was when I was promoted and became the lead person for three of my clients and am able to delegate to and manage others.

Career Goals

I would like to complete my master's degree and move into a research position or lobbying.

Growth Sectors of the Industry for Healthcare Management

Nursing home/assisted living as the baby boom population grows

Professional Role Models and Mentors

My father, who transitioned from a retired Lt. Colonel to a valued consultant, has been my role model.

Knowledge, Skills, Abilities, and Experiences for the Next Generation of Managers

Future managers need to have confidence, possess strong writing and verbal skills, and be driven.

Advice to Students Desiring to Be Future Managers

Step outside of your comfort zone, ask lots of questions, and be thinking of how to differentiate yourself from the person next to you.

REFERENCES

Levy, P. S., & Lemeshow, S. (1980). *Sampling for health professionals.* Belmont, CA: Lifetime Learning Publications.

Locke, E. A. (1983). The nature and causes of job satisfaction. In M. Dunnette (Ed.), *Handbook of industrial and organizational psychology.* New York: John Wiley and Sons, p. 1300.

Longest, B. B., Rakich, J. S, & Darr, K. (2000). *Managing health services organizations and systems.* Baltimore: Health Professions Press.

Vogt, P. W. (1993). *Dictionary of statistics and methodology: A nontechnical guide for the social sciences.* Newbury Park, CA: Sage Publications.

CHAPTER 5

Summary and Conclusions About the Profession

The previous chapter gave you an overview of the practice of healthcare management from the individual perspectives of a variety of healthcare managers. Comments contained in the profiles illustrate managers' thinking about their chosen profession, and provide critical insight into their motivation, satisfaction, challenges, and day-to-day activities. In this chapter, some conclusions about the profession are provided based on the key themes identified in the healthcare manager profiles. In addition, based on the profiles, we provide a summary of key growth areas for healthcare management as well as skills needed by future healthcare managers. Advice for future healthcare managers from these practicing managers is also summarized. We end this chapter with some conclusions about the profession of healthcare management.

THEMES FROM THE HEALTHCARE MANAGER PROFILES

Review of the manager profiles has enabled us to identify several key themes. These key themes reflect interest in the profession and satisfaction; the role of mentors; variation in preparation, experiences, and roles; and challenges faced by healthcare managers. These are discussed below and are highlighted in Table 5.1.

Table 5.1   Key Themes as Identified by Practicing Healthcare Managers

Theme	Findings
Interest in the Profession and Satisfaction	Beyond the larger objectives of helping others, healthcare managers see immense satisfaction in their individual roles and day-to-day task completion.
Role of Mentors	A variety of individuals—peers, bosses, professors, parents, professional colleagues, and preceptors—have been significant sources of influence and have contributed to personal managerial success.
Variation in Preparation, Experiences, and Roles	For managers there are differences in organizations, roles within those organizations, prior work experiences, and educational preparation. There are different paths to the type of career in healthcare management that may interest you.
Challenges Faced by Healthcare Managers	Managers face significant professional challenges coming from internal and external organizational environments.

Interest in the Profession and Satisfaction

Managers have high interest in the healthcare profession and derive significant satisfaction from their roles, despite varying positions, organizations, and backgrounds. A key source of satisfaction is the ability to make a difference in people's lives, even though the day-to-day tasks for managers are typically removed from direct care of individuals. Much reported satisfaction is intrinsic; that is, managers are satisfied with being a part of a healthcare organization and knowing the significance of the work being carried out. A career in healthcare management is rewarding. One manager noted that her role allows for the "combining of compassion with knowledge." Reflecting on her career choice, another realized that "I could make a difference in the lives of others." Another manager recognized through her role that she "had the power to change things for the good of the residents." For many managers, combining an interest in business with the commitment to serving others and improving health care is significant for entering the profession and maintaining day-to-day interest. This is even more remarkable given the significant pressures on managers emanating from internal and external environments, which create ongoing challenges (this is discussed later in this chapter).

Beyond the larger objective of helping others, healthcare managers realize immense satisfaction through their individual roles and day-to-day task completion. Examples of this include working closely with others who share a commitment to the helping profession, being challenged and never being bored in their roles, and having the chance to demonstrate their understanding and key skills in completing tasks and leading others. One manager pointed out that "I know that the work is important and I am working with talented people." Another manager noted that he likes the "self-direction and autonomy to complete what needs to get completed." In addition, learning how to shape relationships with others, creating experiences to grow in knowledge, and having opportunities to explore and advance in positions are all additional sources of satisfaction. These aspects of satisfaction are particularly important for young, entry-level and middle-level managers. Satisfaction is further reinforced by recognition of a job well done. This is illustrated by one manager's comment that "I know that the work is appreciated, and the feeling is great." Another manager noted that "the pace is great and intensity is high, but that it is worth it." While certainly a source of satisfaction, extrinsic factors such as earning competitive compensation and benefits were not mentioned as frequently as the intrinsic sources of satisfaction described above.

What does this mean for you? If you are driven to help others and lead healthcare organizations, then this profession is likely for you. There are many ways to satisfy your intrinsic needs to serve others, work with talented people, and provide health care to those in need. Keep in mind your satisfaction can be realized in different organizational settings and in many different roles. However, the pace is great and complexity is high. Do a self-check and be sure about your overall fit.

The Role of Mentors

Managers report that others—including family, bosses, work colleagues, residency preceptors, professors and professional colleagues, among others—have been significant influences in their lives and have contributed to their personal success. The influence is felt in different ways.

Shared knowledge and expertise help a young manager learn and grow in his or her knowledge and skills. Also, allowing those being mentored to participate in meetings and expand their work activities serves to broaden their knowledge and skills. Through sharing professional values and through modeling of professional and leader behavior, mentors have a significant effect on managers, particularly young managers. By sharing their experiences and life stories, mentors and coaches help managers gain different perspectives on issues based on their own experiences and challenges. Mentors also provide valuable contacts for additional opportunities and career advancement, and provide advice on a wide range of matters. Through encouraging managers to take risks and explore areas of specific interest, mentors have influenced managers to focus on truly meaningful roles and niches within the health services industry.

What does this mean for you? Future managers should seek out individuals to help them along the way. Several managers report serving as mentors now, either formally or informally, and see that role as only more important in the future for successful healthcare management. Many senior managers would gladly serve in the mentor role if asked. We see this as an extension of the healthcare management profession, that is, being part of the "helping profession," and should be something that many senior managers would do to give back.

Variation in Preparation, Experiences, and Roles

Manager profiles reveal differences in organizations, roles within those organizations, experiences, and preparation. The conclusion is that there are different paths to the type of career in healthcare management that you may desire. Many managers began with some exposure to health services while in high school or college, the military services, or through personal or family circumstances with health and disability. Some chose clinical training in college; others chose liberal arts or business and pursued graduate education in healthcare management or business. Some young managers have only a baccalaureate degree and have completed undergraduate degrees in health administration—unavailable to "older" managers when they entered college some years ago.

Part of the appeal of the profession is that there is no single track to the healthcare management position that you desire. Experiences across sectors of the industry are helpful and work to advance one's position and career. Because of the great number and range of managerial opportunities, successful healthcare managers arrive through any number of paths. However, formal knowledge of business, health services, and health services organizations is necessary to becoming a successful healthcare manager and leader.

What does this mean for you? Because of the diversity of opportunities available, healthcare managers can match their specific interests to settings and positions that align with individual career goals. Self-select into those positions that provide the greatest satisfaction based on your specific interests and needs. Be knowledgeable of the educational and experience requirements, as well as the skill expectations, for the positions you are interested in, and design a plan to get where you want to be.

Challenges Faced by Healthcare Managers

Challenges reported by managers include those coming from external environments and those resulting from the internal organizational structure and delivery of services. Externally, cutbacks in reimbursements, intensifying regulations, and the changes that these regulations generate are seen as day-to-day challenges facing direct care organizations. Competition with other organizations is seen as a significant challenge, and it is noted that the pressures for healthcare managers are the same as those for any business (e.g., volume, retention of patients/clients, and revenue/profitability), particularly in down economic cycles. In addition, the lack of understanding among external stakeholders, including policymakers and consumers regarding various sectors of the industry (e.g., assisted living and managed care), is seen as a professional challenge.

Internal professional challenges relate to organizational resources, staff cohesiveness and performance, coordination among staff, organization direction, and personal professional challenges. Limited resources of organizations, including staff shortages and staff turnover, create significant challenges due to the reassignment of work. In addition, both the cost of turnover and the salary expense to hire specialized personnel are reported as significant challenges. Staffing issues such as coworkers who are difficult and employee performance that fluctuates are also important.

Another area of internal challenge relates to the coordination among staff, adapting to changes, and executive leadership. The need to effectively communicate across functions and coordinate activities is critical in healthcare organizations, as well as gaining consensus among management and staff. These issues are highly dependent upon organizational leadership and the ability to articulate and operationalize a vision and direction for the organization. In addition, how the organizational change process is managed and how changes are contemplated, made, and implemented, also present key professional challenges. A final area of professional challenge relates to the personal issues of managers. For example, all managers feel the pressures and time demands to get everything done, as well as the need to solidify personal management effectiveness and organizational skills. In addition, young and mid-career managers wrestle with the challenge of balancing family and career, a pressure felt particularly by many female managers. Moreover, young managers may experience the challenge of finding specific opportunities for growth and advancement within the same organization, and may face the need for movement across organizations to realize personal goals.

What does this mean for you? Be aware of professional challenges associated with the healthcare management positions in which you are most interested, and make sure these challenges do not outweigh the benefits you can realize from your position. Know that there will *always* be challenges, and that you can learn to effectively manage these challenges. Recognize that work-life balance is critical for your personal satisfaction, and determine how you will achieve that in your position and career.

GROWTH AREAS FOR HEALTHCARE MANAGEMENT

Our practicing managers report several key growth areas for healthcare management. These areas include long-term care, elder care, and geriatrics; information technology and data management; Medicare, Medicaid, and other federal health programs; consulting; performance improvement/

quality/patient safety; primary care/ambulatory care; clinical leadership; and reimbursement management in insurer/managed care organizations.

Long-Term Care, Elder Care, and Geriatrics

This area reflects the fact that Americans are living longer and will need a greater numbers of services—inpatient, outpatient, residential, and support—to assist them in having quality of life. Our practicing managers have suggested healthcare management opportunities in nursing homes, assisted living facilities, continuing care retirement communities, and rehabilitation facilities.

Information Technology and Data Management

As the healthcare industry moves to greater use of electronic and computer-driven information technologies and clinical technologies, there are greater opportunities for managers with detailed knowledge, understanding, and skills in managing data as well as in designing and maintaining clinical and financial information systems.

Medicare, Medicaid, and Other Federal Health Programs

This area is seen as an opportunity for growth as more individuals will require public support from Medicare and Medicaid programs in the future. In addition, opportunities in various federal health programs are likely given increasing emphasis on public health, health promotion and improvement, health reporting and accountability, and emergency preparedness and response, as well as new initiatives in reimbursement and pay for performance.

Consulting

There is a need for healthcare managers who can serve as consultants to various healthcare organizations as these organizations deal with pressing problems that affect their competitive position and financial viability.

Performance Improvement/Quality/Patient Safety

With increased pressures on healthcare organizations to improve quality of care, there are opportunities for managers with a detailed understanding of technical and customer services aspects of quality and how to improve their organizations to perform at the highest level of quality.

Primary Care/Ambulatory Care

Recognition of the value of ensuring access to primary care, prevention and early detection, and diagnosis and treatment has created additional management opportunities in primary care and ambulatory care. Managers will work in physician practices, specialty group practices, clinics, HMOs, and other ambulatory care settings to care for the increasing number of Americans who are in need of first contact and preventive care.

Clinical Leadership

Integration of clinical personnel into management positions is seen as a priority by several of our practicing healthcare managers. These leadership areas include nurse leadership and physician leadership. Because healthcare management requires clinical and administrative staff to work closely and effectively, development of nursing and physician leaders is seen as instrumental to boosting organizational performance.

Reimbursement Management in Insurers/Managed Care Organizations

Due to the importance of insurers and managed care organizations in paying for care, opportunities in management in provider reimbursement within these organizations are reported by our practicing managers as a high growth sector in the future.

SKILLS NEEDED FOR THE NEXT GENERATION OF HEALTHCARE MANAGERS

Skills needed for the next generation of healthcare managers as identified by our practicing healthcare managers include:

Customer Service Skills

Be able to recognize that customer service is the primary goal of any health services organization, and that managers must understand how the organization's staff works together to achieve that goal.

Strong Work Ethic and Being Goal Oriented

Work hard to achieve high performance and completion of all required managerial tasks.

Effective Interpersonal and Communications Skills (Oral and Written)

Be able to understand and work with different kinds of people, possess an appreciation of cultural diversity, and have well-developed oral and written communication skills.

Internship/Field Experiences/Volunteerism

Come to the profession with a range of experiences, including volunteer work, paid work, and internships in some areas of the healthcare delivery system, to provide a greater understanding of the field as well as an appreciation of opportunities available.

Be Flexible and Open to New Ideas and Change

Be aware that organizations experience continuous change and that new ways of doing things can be better and more efficient than old ways. As a manager, be open to change and be a change agent. Help the organization evaluate potential changes, and exercise positive change management practices by clarifying the need and benefits of planned changes.

Know How the Healthcare System Works

Regardless of the area you are working in or think you want to work in, develop an awareness and working knowledge of health services delivery in other settings, including the role of non-direct care organizations.

Willingness to Learn

Expand your willingness to learn new things and broaden your understanding of the field, given that the field is changing dramatically.

Passion for This Work

Possess a deep desire and passion to be in health care, and remember why you are in it, particularly when times are rough.

Practice Innovation and Ingenuity, Develop Confidence, and Be Resilient

Be innovative in your thinking and confident in your approach. Know that you will have setbacks and that you will need to develop the capacity of resilience. In all your activities and decisions, be prepared to take away lessons learned from your decisions. As one manager suggests: "Make a decision and learn from it."

Analytical Skills/Finance/Project Management Skills

Because of the deep analytical nature of healthcare management, sharpen your analytical skills (using and analyzing information), your financial analysis skills, and your project management skills. While these skills are technical in nature, keep in mind that you will need to work with a variety of individuals to effectively carry out these technical tasks.

What does this mean for you? If you are serious about this profession, develop these skills where you are lacking, improve these skills where you are weak, and maintain and expand these skills where you are strong.

ADVICE FROM THE MANAGERS

The profiles contain thoughtful and instructive advice for students and young healthcare professionals desiring to be healthcare managers. The advice offered has been categorized into several key areas and is summarized below: engage in experiential learning; work with a mentor; understand motivation, and practice self-awareness and self-management; develop relationship skills; and seek education and lifelong learning.

Engage in Experiential Learning

It is suggested that students and young professionals obtain as much work-related experiences in the health field as possible while a student and in the early phases of their professional career. Such experiences, even if voluntary, create greater understanding of the field and the roles and responsibilities of managers. One manager suggested that an aspiring manager try "different opportunities" to clarify what may be the best fit, or track to take. Try to participate in a variety of experiences and, where possible, include a progression of experience in leadership roles. "Never consider a job to be beneath you," suggests another manager. Be positive about any work experience you are fortunate to have.

Seek Out and Work with a Mentor

Several managers address the value of working with a mentor, where you can learn as much as possible from him or her. Mentoring relationships are very helpful for the future manager to learn about work issues, managing people, and general life lessons. These can be formal relationships, or more commonly, informal relationships where senior managers reach out to younger and less experienced managers who clearly have potential. Seek out a mentor or mentors!

Understand Motivation, and Practice Self-Awareness and Self-Management

As one manager stated, "know thyself." Be sure to understand your motivation to be in this field and be realistic about the enormous rewards and challenges that are part of it. Be passionate about what you are doing, and let that passion come through when serving people—patients, colleagues, and others. "If you have passion about your opportunity," a manager reasons, "it isn't viewed as work—it is viewed as making a difference on a daily basis." "Act with respect, compassion, and caring," another manager advises. Know your strengths and limitations, and seek to provide a balance between your rewarding but demanding work and other parts of your life. But recognize that you will do what it takes to get the job done. A keen summary observation was made by one manager: "Know that you have an impact on patients and employees every day."

Develop Relationship Skills

Develop the knowledge and skills necessary to work effectively with others. This means understanding others' perspectives (i.e., clinical and non-clinical staff), their roles, different functional areas of your organization, and the sectors of the healthcare system. Given the emphasis on working in teams and the leadership roles of managers, aspiring managers should develop and maintain their communication, interpersonal, and organizational skills. Working with and inspiring people are key to being a successful healthcare manager. Develop and practice ethical behavior.

Seek Education and Lifelong Learning

Several managers suggest that future healthcare managers must recognize the value of continuing learning and education. Because of the dynamic nature of the health services field and the profession of healthcare management, an effective healthcare manager requires new knowledge and skills on a continual basis. Join professional associations, take continuing education courses, gain certification by a professional association, take advantage of fellowships and other training opportunities, consider pursuing a master's degree, and identify and network with professional colleagues who can share their knowledge and approaches to help you become a high-performing healthcare manager.

CONCLUSIONS

The field of healthcare management continues to be a growing, rewarding, and challenging profession. This book was written to help you understand the profession of healthcare management—the demand for managers, their roles and responsibilities, key sources of satisfaction, professional challenges, future growth areas for healthcare management, and the necessary skill sets for the next generation of healthcare managers. In addition, it has been written to help you evaluate your own future in healthcare management. In the healthcare manager profiles, you have read about management opportunities in different areas of the health services field and learned from the helpful insights these managers have so graciously shared. Use this book to help shape your own path, recognizing that there are many ways to get to your final destination. Best wishes on your journey! One final note: As academics and past practicing managers, we concur with Richard J. Stull, FACHE, one of our practicing healthcare managers, when he states, "Do it and you will never regret it!"

Resources for Learning More About Healthcare Management

Acronyms, Organizations, and Web Addresses

As the field is growing daily, this list of acronyms, organizations, and website addresses is not intended to be comprehensive, but is provided as a guide for you to find more information about the field of healthcare management.

Acronym	Name of Organization	Website Address
AAAHC	Accreditation Association for Ambulatory Health Care	www.aaahc.org
ACHCA	American College of Health Care Administrators	www.achca.org
ACHE	American College of Healthcare Executives	www.ache.org
ACMPE	American College of Medical Practice Executives	www.mgma.com/ acmpe/index.cfm
AHA	American Hospital Association	www.aha.org
AHIMA	American Health Information Management Association	www.ahima.org
AHIP	America's Health Insurance Plans	www.ahip.org
AHRQ	Agency for Healthcare Research and Quality	www.ahrq.gov

(continued)

Acronym	Name of Organization	Website Address
ALFA	Assisted Living Federation of America	www.alfa.org
AMA	American Medical Association	www.ama-assn.org
APHA	American Public Health Association	www.apha.org
ASAE & The Center	ASAE and the Center for Excellence in Association Leadership	www.asaecenter.org
ASHHRA	The American Society for Healthcare Human Resources Administration	www.ashhra.org
ASTHO	Association of State and Territorial Health Officers	www.astho.org
AUPHA	Association of University Programs in Health Administration	www.aupha.org
BLS	U.S. Bureau of Labor Statistics	www.bls.gov
CAHME	Commission on Accreditation of Healthcare Management Education	www.cahme.org
CARF	Commission on Accreditation of Rehabilitation Facilities	www.carf.org
CMS	Centers for Medicare and Medicaid Services	www.cms.gov
CTS	Center for Studying Health System Change	www.hschange.org
HCC	Health Career Connection	www.healthcareers.org
HFMA	Healthcare Financial Management Association	www.hfma.org
HHS	U.S. Department of Health and Human Services	www.hhs.gov
HIMSS	The Healthcare Information and Management Systems Society	www.himss.org
HRSA	Health Resources and Services Administration	www.hrsa.gov
Institute for Diversity	Institute for Diversity	www.diversityconnection.org
Joint Commission (formerly JCAHO)	The Joint Commission	www.jointcommission.org
KFF	Kaiser Family Foundation	www.kff.org
MGMA	Medical Group Management Association	www.mgma.com
NAB	National Association of Long Term Care Administrator Boards	www.nabweb.org
NACCHO	National Association of County and City Health Officials	www.naccho.org

Acronym	Name of Organization	Website Address
NAHSE	National Association of Health Services Executives	www.nahse.org
NCQA	National Committee for Quality Assurance	www.ncqa.org
NIH	National Institutes of Health	www.nih.gov
PhRMA	Pharmaceutical Research and Manufacturers of America	www.phrma.org
USA.gov	U.S. Government's Official Web Portal	www.firstgov.gov

Sample Bachelor of Science Healthcare Management Programs of Study

James Madison University
Bachelor of Science in Health Services Administration
Course Checklist

General Education Courses

Cluster One:

- ☐ Writing
- ☐ Communication
- ☐ Critical Thinking

Cluster Two:

- ☐ Human Questions and Contexts
- ☐ Visual and Performing Arts Literature

Cluster Three:

- ☐ Statistics
- ☐ Other Track 1 (Science)

Cluster Four:

- □ American Experience
- □ Global Experience

Cluster Five:

- □ Wellness
- □ Sociocultural

BS Degree Requirements

- □ HTH 320 Health Statistics—3 credits. Offered: Fall, Spring, Summer; Prereq: Math 220, HTH 354

  Notes: Math 220 may be taken as part of General Education package or taken separately

- □ HSA 366 Health Politics/Policy—3 credits. Offered: Fall; Prereq: HTH 354 and HSA 365

Required Business Courses (Students receive a Business minor)

- □ COB 204 Computer Information Systems—3 credits. Offered: Fall, Spring

- □ COB 218 Legal Environment of Business—3 credits. Offered: Fall, Spring

- □ COB 241 Financial Accounting—3 credits. Offered: Fall

  Note: Sophomore standing

- □ ECON 201 Principles of Economics—3 credits. Offered: Fall, Spring, Summer

- □ FIN 345 Managerial Finance—3 credits. Offered: Fall, Spring; Prereq: COB 241

  Notes: Junior standing and 2.0 GPA in all JMU courses required

- □ MGT 305 Management and Organizational Behavior—3 credits. Offered: Fall, Spring

  Notes: Junior standing and 2.0 GPA in all JMU courses required

- □ MKTG 380 Principles of Marketing—3 credits offered: Fall, Spring

  Notes: Junior standing and 2.0 GPA in all JMU courses required

Required Health, Gerontology, and Health Services Administration Courses

- ☐ GERN 280 Social Gerontology—3 credits. Offered: Fall, Spring
- ☐ HTH 151 Foundations of Health Science—3 credits. Offered: Fall, Spring
- ☐ HTH 354 U.S. Health Care System—3 credits. Offered: Fall, Spring, Summer

    Note: "B" or better required

- ☐ HSA 358 Health Administration—3 credits. Offered: Fall; Prereq: HTH 354 or instructor permission
- ☐ HSA 363 Health Economics—3 credits. Offered: Fall; Prereq: ECON 201
- ☐ HSA 365 Values in Health Care—3 credits. Offered: Fall, Spring; Prereq: HTH 354 or instructor permission
- ☐ HSA 385 Career Seminar—1 credit. Offered: Fall, Spring
- ☐ HTH 450 Epidemiology—3 credits. Offered: Fall, Spring
- ☐ HSA 454 Internship—3 credits. Offered: Spring, Summer; Prereq: instructor permission

    Notes: Senior standing; 2.5 GPA required in all Health Services Administration courses and a "C" or better required in each course

- ☐ HTH 458 Health Program Planning—3 credits. Offered: Fall, Spring

    Note: Admission to Health Services Administration program required

- ☐ HSA 462 Managed Care—3 credits. Offered: Spring; Prereq: HSA 358 or instructor permission
- ☐ HSA 464 Funding in Health Care—3 credits. Offered: Spring; Prereq: COB 204, COB 241, FIN 345

Choose One of the Following Three Courses:

- ☐ HSA 452 Hospital Organization and Administration—3 credits. Offered: Spring; Prereq: HTH 354, HSA 358
- ☐ HSA 455 Long-Term Care Administration—3 credits. Offered: Spring; Prereq: HTH 354, HSA 358, GERN 280
- ☐ HSA 456 Ambulatory Care Administration—3 credits. Offered: Fall; Prereq: HTH 354, HSA 358

Electives

- ☐ HSA 360 Health Care Marketing—3 credits. Offered: Spring
- ☐ HSA 367 Comparative International Health Systems—3 credits. Offered: every other Spring; Prereq: HTH 354
- ☐ HSA 463 Quality Management—3 credits. Offered: Every other Fall; Prereq: HTH 354, HSA 358
- ☐ Other Electives (7 hours)

Towson University
Healthcare Management Program
Advising Form

The curriculum for the bachelor's degree in Healthcare Management incorporates a multidisciplinary approach. A Business minor is built into the program. Students need only declare the minor when they declare their major. To complete the bachelor's degree, students must satisfy university requirements for graduation (see undergraduate catalog for "Degree Requirements" stipulated within the University Curriculum section). **A grade equivalent of 2.00 or higher must be earned in all courses applied toward the major and minor.**

GENERAL EDUCATION REQUIREMENTS
Skills for Liberal Learning

____ I-A ENGL 102

____ I-B COSC 111 (major prerequisite)

____ I-C MATH 231 (recommended if meet prereq; major prerequisite)

____ I-D ENG 317 (major requirement)

____ I-E Elective Creativity and Creative Development ("your choice")

Scientific Inquiry

____ II-A-I (2 courses; at least one 4-credit lab course)

____ (BIOL 110 recommended)

TOTAL credits: _____

II-A-2 (may be waived if at least 8 credits in IIA1)

American Experience

(*NOTE: Do not take more than 3 courses in same discipline within this category*)

____ II-B-I ("your choice")

HCMN MAJOR REQUIREMENTS
Business Core (21 units)

____ ACCT 201 Accounting Principles I (3)

____ ACCT 202 Accounting Principles II (3)

____ COSC 111 Information and Technology for Business (3)

____ ECON 201 Microeconomic Principles (3)

____ ECON 202 Macroeconomic Principles (3)

____ ECON 339 Health Economics (3)

____ ENGL 317 Writing for Business and Industry (3)

____Laboratory Science Elective (3, 4)

____ FIN 331 Financial Management (3)

____ LEGL 225 Legal Environment of Business (3)

____ MNGT 361 Principles of Management (3)

____ MKTG 341 Principles of Marketing (3)

____ MATH 231 Basic Statistics (3)

Required Courses
Healthcare Management (21 units)

____ HLTH 101 Current Health Problems (3)

____ HLTH 207 Health Care in the U.S. (3)

____ HCMN 305 Healthcare Administration (3)

____ HLTH 311 Chronic and Communicable Disease (3)

____ HCMN 413 Services and Housing for the Long-Term Care Consumer

(continued)

**GENERAL EDUCATION
REQUIREMENTS
Skills for Liberal Learning**

**HCMN MAJOR REQUIREMENTS
Business Core (21 units)**

American Experience (*cont.*)

____ II-B-3 HLTH 101 (major prerequisite)

Western Heritage

____ II-C-1 ("your choice")

____ *II-C-2 ECON 201 (minor requirement)

____ *II-C-2 GERO 101 (major prerequisite)

____ *II-C-2 Two courses from different disciplines are required in this category

____ *II C-3 ("your choice")

Global Awareness

____ II-D ("your choice")

____ HCMN 415 Finance and Organization of Health Care in the U.S. (3)

____ HCMN 441 Legal and Ethical Issues in Health Administration (3)

____ GERO 101 Introduction to Gerontology (3)

*____ **Internship-HCMN 495 (12 units) REQUIRED**

Additional Courses

____ Long-Term Care Track (12 units) OPTIONAL

____ HCMN 417 Long-Term Care Ethical Problems (3)

HCMN 419 Long-Term Care Administration (3)

HLTH 411 Health and Later Maturity—The Aging Process (3)

---

*Students have the opportunity to gain hands-on, practical work experience in this required full-term capstone course. Students will be able to apply the knowledge and skills they have acquired in managing and delivering health services. Students must apply for the internship in the term prior to enrolling in HCMN 495. The internship coordinator will assign students to a placement site based on the acceptability of student to the agency and the acceptability of the agency to student.

Towson University
Healthcare Management Program
Typical Sequence of Required Courses and
Commonly Taken Electives

YEAR ONE

Semester 1	Credits	Semester 2	Credits
ENGL 102 (IA)	3	COSC 111 (IB)	3
MATH 111 (IC)	3	BIOL 110 (IIA 1)	4
OR		MATH 231	3
MATH 115 (IC)		HLTH 207	3
HLTH 101 (IIB 3)	3	ECON 201 (IIC 2)	3
GERO 101 (IIC 2)	3		
GenEd IE	3		
Semester Total Credits	**15**	Semester Total Credits	**16**
Semester 1		**Semester 2**	
ACCT 201	3	ACCT 202	3
2nd Lab Science IIA 1	4	ECON 202	3
HLTH 311	3	GenEd IIC 1	3
LEGL 225	3	GenEd IID	3
GenEd IIB 1	3	HCMN 305	3
Semester Total Credits	**16**	Semester Total Credits	**15**
Semester 1		**Semester 2**	
FIN 331	3	HCMN 413	3
MNGT 361	3	MKTG 341	3
ENG 317 (ID)	3	HCMN 441	3
ECON 339	3	GenEd IIC 3	3
HCMN 415	3	Elective	3
Semester Total Credits	**15**	Semester Total Credits	**15**
Semester 1		**Semester 2**	
HCMN 417	3	HCMN 495	12
HCMN 419	3	HLTH 497 Professional	1
HLTH 411	3	Development	
Elective	3		
Elective	3		
Semester Total Credits	**15**	Semester Total Credits	**13**
		TOTAL CREDITS	**120**

Sample Master of Health Administration (MHA) Degree Requirements

The Pennsylvania State University

The MHA program is designed to be completed in 21 months of full-time study, although it may be completed on a part-time basis. A minimum of 49 credits is required for completion of the degree. Students take 43 credits of required courses. In addition, 6 credits of electives are selected in consultation with an advisor.

YEAR ONE				
Semester 1		**Credits**	**Semester 2**	**Credits**
HPA 447	Financing Health Care	3	HPA 524 Management of Health Services Organizations	3
HPA 503	Understanding Organizational Behavior	3	HPA 536 Health Law	3
HPA 520	Introduction to Health Organizations and Policy	3	HPA 528 Health Data Analysis	3
HPA 897B	Processes of Health and Disease	3	HPA 535 Financial Management in Health Institutions *Prerequisite: HPA 447*	3

(continued)

YEAR ONE (cont.)

Semester 1	Credits	Semester 2	Credits
Semester Total Credits	12	Semester Total Credits	12
SUMMER			
HPA 595 Graduate Residency*	1		

YEAR TWO

Semester 3	Credits	Semester 4	Credits
HPA 897A Processes of Planned Change	3	HPA 555 Information Systems in Health Services Administration	3
HPA 545 Introduction to Health Economics	3	HPA 556 Strategy Development in Health Services Organization	3
HPA 523 Managerial Epidemiology	3	HPA 597 Quality Improvement in Health Care	3
HPA 897E Healthcare Marketing	3	Electives	3
Semester Total Credits	12	Semester Total Credits	12
		TOTAL CREDITS	**49**

*Graduate Residency: During the summer between the first and second academic years, MHA students are required to obtain and carry out a 10-week graduate administrative residency. It is the student's responsibility to identify and arrange the administrative residency, in consultation with the executive director of the MHA program.

Getting a Job in Healthcare Management

Frequently Asked Questions (FAQs)

Q: I was thinking about becoming a nurse, but I don't like chemistry or biology. Does healthcare management (HCMN) require life science courses?

A: To earn a BS or BA in HCMN, universities and colleges require students to complete General Education requirements, which may include life science courses.

Q: My mom is a nurse, her mom was a nurse, my aunt is a nurse, and they want me to be a nurse, too. I want to help people, but I don't want to touch them! What can I tell my family?

A: Tell your family that healthcare management is just as sacred as nursing and medicine. As a healthcare manager, you will be working side-by-side with nurses and physicians, making sure resources get to clinicians to provide the needed services to patients. It will be your responsibility to balance access, costs, and quality of care—and it is always about the patient, client, or resident.

Q: I live in a small town in a rural state. How can I find an HCMN program that works for me?

A: The Association of University Programs in Health Administration (www.aupha.org) has a listing of undergraduate and graduate programs in HCMN available at http://www.aupha.org/i4a/pages/index .cfm?pageid=3357. In addition, there is a searchable directory on the AUPHA website with information on baccalaureate, master's, doctoral, executive, and continuing education programs, along with information on admissions, estimated costs, and a geographic index.

Q: How long will it take me to get through an undergraduate HCMN program?

A: Most undergraduate programs require 120 credits to graduate. Generally speaking, if you are able to take 30 credits a year, you can complete a BS/BA in HCMN in 4 years. How rapidly you progress will be determined by your ability to do well in the courses, options to take courses during the summer, or how often the program offers courses for its majors.

Q: I work full time and support my family. I cannot go to school full time. Are there any part time or online programs available in HCMN?

A: Yes and yes! More and more "bricks and mortar" schools are offering both part-time programs with offerings in the evenings and on weekends, as well as online courses. In addition, there are a number of excellent online programs in HCMN at both the undergraduate and graduate levels. Many of these are listed on the AUPHA website at http://www.aupha.org/i4a/pages/index.cfm?pageid=3641.

Q: How much money will I make when I graduate?

A: As noted in Chapter 3 of this book, salaries will vary by setting, size of organization, number of employees, geographic locale, and your education and level of experience. That said, on average, entry-level graduates with a BS/BA can expect to earn between $32,000 and $40,000 per year. People with a master's degree and above in senior executive positions can earn six-figure incomes.

Q: What is an internship or residency, and why should I do one?

A: At the undergraduate level, internships provide you with the opportunity to transition from a student role to a professional role and enable you to find a part of healthcare management you really like—or don't like. Internships are opportunities for networking with potential employers, learning more information about the niche you are interested in, and provide you with a potential job reference if you do well. At the graduate level, residencies offer the same kinds of opportunities as internships, but at a more senior level, with an executive mentor who serves as your professional development coach. These 6-month-to-year-long practicums are often paid, making it an affordable choice for many.

Q: I'm thinking about going to law school. Is this a good major for me?

A: HCMN provides you with a solid base of understanding of how health care works in the United States. Many students who graduate with degrees in HCMN go on for advanced education—some go to law school, some to dental or medical school, and others go to nursing school. A number of HCMN Master's programs offer joint degrees with MBAs, JDs, MPHs, or other degrees. The opportunities for leveraging a degree in HCMN are many.

Q: I'm currently working in a hospital as an administrative coordinator where I have worked for 3 years, and I would really like to get into consulting or pharmaceutical sales. Can I do this?

A: Yes. The experience you have gained in the hospital setting is transferable to the settings you have interest in. The administrative tasks and responsibilities that you have carried out are similar to those required in the new settings of interest. Consulting and pharmaceutical sales positions require strong personal motivation and self-direction, and well-developed communication and interpersonal skills. If you possess these skills, and if opportunities are available in consulting and pharmaceutical sales where you would like to live, this could be an excellent move for you given your past experience.

Q: I have just graduated from college with a BS in Healthcare Management and am worried about my first job because I am not sure what specific setting I really like. I am concerned that I might go down the "wrong track" by eliminating other options. What should I do?

A: Many new graduates are concerned about their first jobs because there is much uncertainty associated with beginning a professional career and completing the transition to the "world of work." As noted in this book, you first need to identify your interests and needs. The appeal of the healthcare management profession is that there are many opportunities available and that you can move from one setting or sector to another. Your first position, regardless of its nature, will provide excellent work experience and give you a chance to further clarify your interests and needs while helping to develop your professional knowledge and skills. Recognize that you will not be in this first position forever. Consider it a stepping stone to other management opportunities, and learn what you like and don't like about particular settings and roles within this field based on your experience in your first position. You have many options.

Commonly Used Terms in Job Advertising and Position Descriptions

When you see a job listing, position announcement, or position description, you may find that there are several terms used that sometimes are unclear. While the following terms and their definitions are not intended to be comprehensive, they should prove useful to you when reading various job announcements and position descriptions in healthcare management.

Position Title: This describes the managerial position. Every position in a healthcare organization has a specific title.

Department: The organizational unit where the position is located.

Reporting Line: This term refers to the person who supervises the position on a daily basis and evaluates the performance of the person in the position. For example, the marketing coordinator for a hospital may report to the director of marketing and business development, who assigns work to the marketing coordinator, monitors the marketing coordinator's performance, and evaluates the marketing coordinator's performance at least on an annual basis.

Summary of Responsibilities: This section is a description of the areas of responsibility assigned to, and the specific roles and tasks carried out by, the person occupying the position. In addition, the duties and responsibilities may specify the manager's working relationships with other functional areas of the organization. For example, the activities director of a nursing home or assisted living facility is responsible for identifying and developing activities to meet the needs of residents by working closely with nursing and rehabilitation staff, and ensuring that these programs are provided to the residents in a systematic way to meet their physical, cognitive, and social needs. Another example would be a director of research for a hospital system who is responsible for designing, leading, and supervising research studies relating to the system's services and patient outcomes, and who will work with administrative and clinical managers and staff in providing guidance in quantitative and qualitative research of administrative and clinical data.

Qualifications, or Education, Training, and Experience: These terms refer to the specific qualifications (requirements) in terms of education, training, and experience necessary to successfully carry out the job.

Education: The minimum level of college degree (BA/BS, master's, doctorate) required for the position. The required education level will vary with the type and scope of responsibilities for the position. Educational requirements may also stipulate the major field of study necessary for the job (e.g., Health Administration, Informatics, Finance, etc.).

Training: Any special certification, registration, or licensure will be specified (e.g., Registered Nurse licensure, licensed nursing home administrator, or Registered Records Administrator). Other specific training requirements will be described here.

Experience: The completion of prior work that is required for a position (e.g., 2 years project management experience and an overall knowledge of healthcare delivery and healthcare policy). Experience may be required in specific positions and or in specific organizational settings (e.g., hospital, physician practice, nursing home, etc.).

Special Skills or Other Requirements: This contains the specific knowledge, as well as conceptual, analytic/technical, and interpersonal skills, required for the job (e.g., excellent oral and written communication skills and ability to perform several tasks/projects simultaneously; proficiency with Windows-based word processing and spreadsheet applications).

Supervisory Responsibilities: This refers to the positions that are supervised and evaluated by the person occupying the managerial position.

Key Work Relationships: This specifies the other administrative, clinical, and support units that the manager works with on a regular basis to carry out the responsibilities and required activities for the position.

Additional Terms Used in Position Announcements

Equal Opportunity Employer/Women, Minorities, and Those Needing Accommodation Are Encouraged to Apply: This refers to the fact that the organization is an "Equal Opportunity Employer," meaning that all persons who meet the qualifications for the position are encouraged to apply and will be considered, regardless of their sex, ethnicity/national origin, race, disability, age, and so on. It is important for health services organizations to mirror the communities they serve, and so therefore it is important that all qualified persons be considered in the screening, evaluation, and hiring process.

Compensation: This describes salary or wages for the position, in terms of an absolute amount or a range. This is presented based on a yearly amount (i.e., annual salary) or presented based on an hourly wage rate (i.e., paid by the hour).

Benefits: The advertisement may describe benefits associated with the position (other than salary or wages). Benefits may include time off (e.g., sick leave, vacation, holidays), insurance (e.g., health, disability, life, and long-term care insurance), retirement or pension plan (i.e., 401K plan, 403B plan), tuition assistance for college, continuing education, travel allowance, child care assistance, and dependent care and healthcare flexible spending/reimbursement accounts, among others.

References: This refers to the persons you list for the potential employer to contact regarding your knowledge, skills, experiences, and performance. Be sure to carefully select your professional references by choosing those individuals who view you favorably, and are likely to report positive things about you. Also, make sure that your chosen references have agreed in advance to serve as a reference, and be sure to remind them at the time you submit an application that they may receive a call or e-mail about you from a prospective employer. Make certain that contact information for the reference is current and correctly listed (see Checklist for Finding the Right Job below).

Application Process: This describes the requirements for preparing and submitting an application for the advertised position. Be sure to follow all requirements and complete and submit the necessary paperwork, including a résumé, by the submission deadline. If an online application process is used, make sure that you receive a confirmation on your submission and print out a copy of your application and note on it the day and time submitted.

Sample Position Descriptions

FRIENDLY MEDICAL CENTER, INC.

Position Description

Position Title: Managed Care Coordinator

Department: Finance

Reports to: Vice President of Finance

Summary of Responsibilities: The managed care coordinator is responsible for coordinating all managed care activities of the Medical Center, including developing contract proposals for submission to managed care organizations/insurers; evaluating contract proposals from managed care organizations/insurers; monitoring managed care contract performance; planning, and conducting negotiations on behalf of the Medical Center; maintaining the managed care contracts inventory and database; and maintaining timely and effective communications with contracted health plans/insurance companies. Responsibilities for managed care contracting and negotiations extend to Medical Center-owned physician practices, and to physicians who are employed by the Medical Center. In addition, the managed care coordinator will carry out other assigned duties and assignments as requested by the vice president of finance.

Education, Training, and Experience: Master's degree in Health Administration, Business, or a related field. Five years experience in insurance and/or third-party contracting within a hospital or hospital system, or 5 years experience in a marketing, sales, or contracting role within an HMO, PPO, or health insurer.

Special Skills or Other Requirements: Strong computer and analytic skills with proficiency in spreadsheet and data manipulation and analysis, word processing, and presentation software. Strong communications skills with the ability to communicate clearly and persuasively in oral and written form. Strong interpersonal and sales skills with the ability to effectively conduct and finalize negotiations with managed care organizations/insurers.

Supervisory Responsibilities: Supervises the managed care analyst and administrative assistant, managed care.

Key Work Relationships: Marketing, medical staff support services, Medical Center-affiliated physicians, employed physicians, and physician office staff.

FRIENDLY MEDICAL CENTER, INC.

Position Description

Position Title: Senior Planning Analyst

Department: Marketing and Business Development

Reports to: Vice President of Marketing and Business Development

Summary of Responsibilities: The senior planning analyst is responsible for coordinating the strategic planning for the Medical Center, including identifying community health needs, conducting internal and external assessments, and working with administration in finalizing the strategic plan and its annual updates. In this role, the senior planning analyst monitors external trends and influences in the Medical Center's services area; profiles and analyzes competitor organizations' services, strategies, and plans; establishes and projects trend data on service lines of the Medical Center; identifies, in conjunction with other administrative leaders, capital expenditures and other planned developments requiring Certificate of Need (CON); prepares CON applications and submits to appropriate external agencies as necessary; and maintains the Medical Center's Planning Database in support of organizationwide and service line planning efforts. Responsibilities for planning extend to Medical Center-owned physician practices, and other Medical Center-owned business units, including the Ambulatory Surgery Center, Skilled Nursing Facility, and Wellness Center. In addition, the senior planning analyst will carry out other assigned duties and assignments as requested by the vice president of marketing and business development.

Education, Training, and Experience: Bachelor's degree in Health Administration with 5 years of responsible experience in planning and analysis in a hospital, other healthcare organization, or consulting firm; *or* a master's degree in Health Administration, Business, Planning, or a related field, and 3 years experience in planning, analysis, or business development in a hospital, hospital system, consulting firm, or other healthcare organization.

Special Skills or Other Requirements: Strong computer and analytic skills with proficiency in spreadsheet and data manipulation and analysis, including data file merging, and word processing and presentation software. Ability to work with large and complex data sets. Strong communications skills with the ability to communicate clearly and persuasively in oral and written form. Strong interpersonal skills with the ability to effectively work with a wide variety of internal and external stakeholders.

Supervisory Responsibilities: Supervises the planning analyst, the planning information systems analyst, and the administrative assistant, planning.

Key Work Relationships: Marketing, service line managers, medical staff support services, subsidiary business unit managers, and Medical Center-owned physician practices.

Do's and Don'ts of Interviewing

Job interviews are stressful, at best, and can be nightmares, at worst. As with most things, one way you can reduce stress is to prepare and practice your job interviewing skills. Just as you can learn how to be a better public speaker, you can learn how to be a better job candidate in a face-to-face interview. As the saying goes, you don't get a second chance to make a good first impression. The following are some tried-and-true tips as you prepare for the starring role of your life: Best candidate for the job!

Do's

- *Research the organization.* You should do this at every step along the way, from finding out where the jobs are listed, networking with people in the field, and writing that pitch-perfect cover letter. Do you have friends or family members who work there? Ask them what will make you a successful candidate for the job. Almost every healthcare organization has a website. Read and review the organization's values, mission, vision, and goals. And, try to determine where you will fit in. You should be able to answer questions from why you chose this organization to where you expect to see yourself in the next 10 years. Be certain that every response you give echoes the organization's position in the marketplace. Interviewers are looking for people who understand the firm and want to know if you will fit in. You need to be able to articulate what you will bring to the job that is unique, refreshing, and important to the mission of the organization.
- *Practice your interviewing skills.* Most campus communities have Career Centers to assist students in job searches. Even if you have

graduated, alumni are usually welcome to return and utilize their services. This is the time to practice your handshake and eye contact. Nothing beats real-world experience. Try to go on a few job interviews before you go to the one you are most concerned about. Additionally, more and more job interviews are being conducted by telephone and remote interview. You may be asked to videotape an interview, or to meet in cyberspace with a webcam. Practice the technology before you go live so you will be comfortable and relaxed. The keys to effective interviews: be positive, enthusiastic, and relaxed.

- *Dress the part for the job you want.* Generally speaking, the healthcare management field has a conservative culture. Before you go for an interview, take a look at the way people are dressed on websites that are representative of healthcare executives, such as the American College of Healthcare Executives (www.ache.org), the Medical Group Management Association (www.mgma.com), and the American Hospital Association (www.aha.org). You will not see men in baseball caps, jeans, tee-shirts, and flip-flops. Nor will you see women with exposed cleavage, uncovered belly buttons, or low-rider jeans. You will see men dressed in dark suits, dress shirts, and ties. If you do not own a suit, you must buy one, or (for men) have at least a sport jacket with khakis, to be considered a serious job-seeker. Women need to wear suits, too, and although there is more variability in styles and color, you should wear a dark suit for the interview.

- *Practice getting to the interview.* Make a practice run at the same time of day that you will be having the actual interview, and plan to arrive at least 15 minutes ahead of time. Few things in life are more frustrating or frazzling than having an important appointment and running late. Not only will you be frantic when you arrive, your potential employer will take a dim view of your tardiness. Better to arrive too early than too late.

- *Ask thoughtful questions.* Although you are being judged to see whether you fit the organization, this is your opportunity to assess if this organization is the one for you. Some questions that you might ask include: "What happened to the last person in this position?" "Are there opportunities for continuing education so I can keep up with the field?" and "Where do you see the organization 5 years from now?" Asking thoughtful questions signals that you have given much thought to the position you are interested in, and that you have prepared for the interview.

- *Bring extra copies of your résumé and cover letter.* Paperwork can be misplaced and sometimes one interviewer morphs into a group interview with five people staring at you. Bring extra handouts of anything you plan to discuss, whether it's your résumé, portfolio projects, or writing samples.
- *Alert your references.* Let your references know that you have an interview, the date of the interview, and with whom, so they can be prepared for a phone call or e-mail from your prospective employer. It is a good habit to keep your references informed of the progress on your job search. You never know—one might hear of a job opening that's perfect for you.

Don'ts

- *Do not wait until the last minute.* Whether it is making sure you have a clean outfit to wear, finding your way to the interview site, or updating your résumé, be prepared *ahead* of time. Knowing that you have everything under control will reduce your anxiety.
- *Do not wear excessive makeup, perfume, aftershave, or jewelry.* The simpler the better. Shower the day of the interview and use a good deodorant. Many people have allergies to fragrances, and some organizations have declared themselves "Fragrance Free Zones." Likewise, excessive makeup may call up concerns about your expectations of the work environment. You don't want your prospective employer to think that you plan to go out and party every night. With respect to jewelry, a watch (for a man) and a watch, a pearl necklace, and earrings (for women) are elegant, understated, and professional.
- *Do not expose body art (tattoos) or multiple body piercings.* Although is it widely recognized that Generation X and beyond have more body art and piercings than their parents, and these choices are acceptable among their peers, the person making the hiring decision is likely to be your parents' age—not your age. The rule of tattoos is if you plan to become a healthcare executive and you want body art, then you should keep it all above your wrists and below your shirt collar. Likewise, tongue piercings, especially ones that cause speech problems, are extremely distracting and will not endear you to the interviewer. While multiple ear piercings are more acceptable now, the rule of thumb for women is not to exceed two per earlobe. For men, ear piercings are strongly discouraged at job interviews. Ditto eyebrow,

nose, and lip piercings for men and women. Piercings will rarely "grow over" in the course of a day. If you are concerned, you can purchase and insert retainers to prevent the piercings from growing over.

- *Do not put anything on social networking sites that will damage your future job opportunities.* Employers who are seriously considering job applicants can and will run background checks on you. The first place they will look is on the Internet. If they search on your name, what will they find? Will it be pictures or video files of you clearly under the influence of alcohol or drugs? Will you be seen making obscene gestures or heard using language that would make a sailor blush? Clean up your act and your Internet websites. And remember, once something is published on an Internet blog, unless you own the blog and can take it down, it lives there *forever.*

- *Do not allow past indiscretions to ruin your future.* If you have a criminal record, a potential employer will find it. Don't kid yourself into thinking that no one will find that marijuana charge from your high school senior week at the ocean. In healthcare settings, a criminal background check is almost always required for employment. Criminal background checks can be run inexpensively and *quickly.* If you have kept out of trouble for 3 years, in most states you can have your criminal record sealed or expunged. Usually you must go to the courthouse where you were convicted, complete the application requesting expungement, and pay a fee. This process can take anywhere from 3 months to a year, depending on how busy the court docket is and how involved your record is. Since we are not lawyers, we strongly urge you to seek legal counsel for assistance and start the process as soon as you are eligible to do so.

- *Do not use drugs or arrive at your interview under the influence of alcohol, drugs, or smelling of cigarettes.* While addiction is a disease, employers do not want to hire people with addictions who are actively using and not in recovery. Usually a job offer is made pending the successful completion of drug testing and any other preemployment tests deemed to be of importance. Many healthcare employers require physical examinations, and blood and other types of tests, such as tine tests for tuberculosis. This is the time to reconsider smoking, recreational drug use, and all other substances that might have become part of your lifestyle. Your campus health center can be an excellent resource for information on how to quit smoking. In addition, there are national organizations available, such as Alcoholics Anonymous (www.aa.org) and Narcotics Anonymous (www.na.org), with meetings all over the world, face-to-face, and online.

Checklist for Finding the Right Job

One thing to realize about getting the job you want is that you need to have a *strategy* for getting that job. The following is a checklist of steps to follow. Also, remember that you are likely to have several different jobs in your healthcare career as you progress in the scope of responsibilities and types of positions you hold over time. Many young professionals— particularly those coming right out of school—worry about making a mistake by selecting the wrong first position. Try not to be paralyzed by worrying about making a wrong choice. The fact is that the first position will be helpful to you in building your experiences and clarifying your next steps in healthcare management, and therefore is rarely a misstep.

- *Decide on setting and type of job you want.* Do your homework and determine those settings and positions that represent a match based on your interests and needs. Research the setting and specific organizations within that setting where you would like to work.
- *Develop a résumé and cover letter.* Develop a concise résumé that indicates your work objective, and specifies your education, experience, special skills, and certification/licensure. Customize a cover letter that you can use later to apply for positions in that setting.
- *Determine available positions and apply for jobs.* This step is the most challenging. Most jobs that you will be interested in are not advertised in usual media (i.e., newspapers, journals). You should check available positions listed online at websites such as www.Monster.com and www.longtermcarecareers.org, as well as the human resources section of websites of health organizations you are interested in. It is more effective to find out about jobs by networking. Contact and send your résumé to professionals you may know who are working in the field; administrators you have met, worked for, or volunteered for; former professors who may know of opportunities; and family members who either work in the field or know of someone who works in the field. Develop a plan for identifying and following up with contacts. Your

objective is to narrow down potential positions in settings you like. Even though people you network with may not have any available positions, they frequently are a valuable source of knowledge of other opportunities or individuals you can contact. Once you identify a position of interest, obtain a copy of the position description and/or job summary, and make sure that the job fits your interest and needs, and that you meet the job qualifications. Make the proper applications for positions you are interested in, which are likely to require you to submit your résumé and customized cover letter.

- *Interview.* Go on as many interviews as possible—this builds experience and confidence. Practice your interviewing skills so that you can interview well (see Do's and Don'ts of Interviewing above). Provide carefully chosen references for yourself, and make sure that you have asked each of your references in advance for their agreement to be a reference for you. Provide accurate and current contact information for your references.

- *Narrow your search.* Based on your interviewing experiences, decide which opportunities best meet your interests and needs, and rank your possibilities. Be prepared to say "no" to some and "yes" to others, if you are offered a position.

- *Evaluate offers.* Be clear on the specific job offer. Make sure that you understand the compensation, benefits (including various types of health insurance, paid time off, retirement plan, savings plans, education tuition reimbursement policy, etc.), and work requirements and expectations. Be sure to get the offer in writing and make sure that it reflects your expectations based on what you have been told and what you have read in the position description. Keep in mind that all offers are negotiable. If there are some aspects of the job that you feel are not adequate (i.e., salary, work hours per week, etc.), try to negotiate these aspects of the job. Before negotiating, talk with others whom you trust and who may have knowledge about the adequacy of the offer (e.g., friends, colleagues, and professors), and gain their advice. Accept an offer in writing.

- *Follow up.* Be sure to send thank you notes to those people who have helped you along the way—network contacts, references, and persons with whom you have interviewed. This is extremely important and reflects positively on your professionalism.

Sample Cover Letters and Résumés

Sample Cover Letter and Résumé: BS in Healthcare Management

Ivonna Work

555 Your Street
Your Town, Your State Your Zip Code
(555)555-5555
IvonnaWork@xyxmail.com

Month, Day, Year

Joyce Oaks
Human Resource Director
Fair Oaks Nursing and Rehabilitation Center
555 Fair Oaks Way
Fair Oaks, CT 12345

Dear Ms. Oaks:

I am writing in response to the position I found online today at www.longtermcarecareers.org for a payroll/AP coordinator for your 150-bed skilled nursing facility, Fair Oaks Nursing and Rehabilitation Center. Your website indicates that your turnover among full-time employees is less than 2% per year and almost half of your staff has been employed at your facility for 5 years or longer. I know that these numbers indicate that you have a satisfied staff, and I am very interested in working in your collaborative environment.

I see from your posting that you are looking for someone with a minimum of 1 year's experience in payroll processing, ledger and accounts payable. I also note that long-term care experience is strongly preferred. As noted in the requirements, I am very familiar with the All Time System and have been responsible for employee benefits enrollments and other human resources functions, as well as accounts payable and other bookkeeping duties. I believe I have all the qualifications you seek, plus enthusiasm, attention to detail, accountability, integrity, passion for my work, and compassion for the elderly.

As you can observe from my enclosed résumé, I have a BS in Healthcare Management, a minor in Business Administration, and a track in Long-Term Care. Upon completion of my full-time, 12-credit internship at St. Thomas More Home and Rehabilitation Center, I was hired to be the payroll coordinator for this 216-bed skilled nursing facility. I have enjoyed my work at St. Thomas More Home and Rehabilitation Center here in Maryland, and have had increased responsibility over the past year, however, my husband and I would like to be closer to our families in Connecticut.

I would like to arrange a meeting with you in December, when I will be in Fair Oaks. I can be reached by e-mail at IvonnaWork@xyxmail.com

Sincerely,

Ivonna Work

Ivonna Work

555 Your Street
Your Town, Your State, Your Zip Code
(555)555-5555 (Cell)
IvonnaWork@xyxmail.com

Education

Towson University, Towson, Maryland

- BS, Healthcare Management, Minor in Business Administration, Track in Long-Term Care, December, 2007
- Member, Upsilon Phi Delta, HCMN Honor Society
- Resident Assistant 2006–2007

Experience

December 2007–Present
St. Thomas More Nursing Home and Rehabilitation Center, Hyattsville, Maryland

Payroll Coordinator
- Maintain payroll records and files
- Set up payroll deductions such as garnishments, levy, and adjustments to benefits
- Assist in the administration of time and attendance records
- Assist in the balancing of quarterly and annual state, federal, and FICA tax reports
- Address questions and concerns pertaining to paychecks and payroll hours
- Data entry in OSI and Unitime systems
- Process payroll and ensure that employee time card hours are accurate
- Input new hires' tax information into OSI; and ensure they are correctly set up on the time clock and Unitime system
- Generate payroll reports

September 2007–December 2007
St. Thomas More Nursing Home and Rehabilitation Center, Hyattsville, Maryland

Intern: Worked in numerous departments within the faculty but primarily worked in the Minimum Data Set (MDS) department.

January 2007–May 2007
Towson University, Towson, MD

Tutor: Tutored students in kindergarten and 4th grade at Patapsco Elementary in Baltimore City, Maryland

November 2005–May 2006
Towson University, Towson, Maryland—Office of Assessment

Office Assistant: Clerical duties including typing, filing, copying, phone and reception, mailings, scheduling, and related work. Administrative support duties including project tracking, file management, routine correspondence, and events support.

References: Available upon request

Sample Cover Letter and Résumé: Master of Health Administration

David Hardworker

555 XYZ Street, Your City, Your State, Your Zip Code

Month, Day, Year

Recruiter
ABC Healthcare
555 Healthcare Street
Healthcare City, MD 12345

Dear Sir/Madam:

I am writing in response to the position I found online today at www
.monster.com for a senior sales representative to assist with business
development in major cities in the United States. Your website indicates
that ABC Healthcare has serviced more than 4,000 clients in all 50
states and throughout the world, and that your clients include hospitals,
health systems, integrated delivery networks, and other providers of
care; payers and health plans; life sciences and technology firms; and
federal government agencies. I was excited to see the depth and breadth
of opportunities with your firm, and am very interested in working in
your team environment.

I see from your posting that you are looking for someone with professional
experience with a range from a minimum of 5 to 10 years of healthcare
experience and a general understanding of healthcare provider operations
and issues. In addition, you note the candidate must possess a level of
formal and professional education commensurate with the demands of the
position.

As you can see from my enclosed résumé, I have a BS in Healthcare
Management and a Master of Health Administration from The
Pennsylvania State University. In addition to my 6 years of education in
Healthcare Management, over the past 3 years I have been working in a
variety of healthcare settings, including ambulatory care and hospital,
employing all types of sales strategies, including cold calls, for software
sales and marketing. I am an excellent communicator, with strong verbal
and written skills, as demonstrated by my graduate teaching assistantship.
I am extremely organized, able to multitask, and know the Delmarva

region. I enjoy teamwork and am proficient in various computer software programs, such as Excel and Access. I believe I have all the qualifications you seek, plus enthusiasm, attention to detail, accountability, integrity, passion for my work, and I enjoy working with healthcare providers.

I would like to arrange a meeting with you in December. I can be reached by e-mail at DavidHardworker@xyxmail.com

Sincerely,

David Hardworker

David Hardworker

555 XYZ Street, Your City, Your State, Your Zip Code

E-mail: davehardworker@xyxmail.com • (555)555-5555

Education

September 2005–May 2007

The Pennsylvania State University, University Park, PA

Master of Health Administration, The College of Health and Human Development

- Degree Awarded: May 2007—GPA 3.7/4.0

January 2003–May 2005

Towson University, Towson, MD

Bachelor of Science in Healthcare Management, Minor in Business

- Degree Awarded: May 2005—GPA 3.4/4.0

Healthcare Experience

August 2007–October 2008

MDLogix, Baltimore, MD: *Assistant to the Vice President of Marketing*

- Contacted potential clients to determine whether they are in need of MDLogix's software products and services
- Gave initial presentation to potential clients who have an interest in MDLogix's main software product, a Clinical Research Management System
- Conducted research on bids and proposals put out by universities and other organizations that are in need of a Clinical Research Management System
- Assisted in editing proposals so that they are suitable for submission
- Assisted the QA department by testing the MDLogix software products

May 2006–July 2006

Suburban Hospital, Bethesda, MD: *Administrative Resident, Medical Staff Office*

- Gathered and organized physician quality/utilization data from various hospital departments to be analyzed at time of physician reappointment

- Conducted an extensive cost/benefit analysis on physician credentialing software packages
- Developed an efficient process to collect physician dues
- Gave presentations based on the above projects to senior management

January 2005–May 2005

Mosaic Community Services, Timonium, MD: *Administrative Intern*

- Compiled revenue/cost data for Mosaic's patients and developed a detailed cost analysis report
- Conducted research to help determine whether the company should expand into a federally qualified health center

Other Experience

September 2005–May 2007

The Pennsylvania State University, University Park, PA: *Graduate Teaching Assistant*

- Led weekly discussion based on relevant healthcare topics
- Met with students to assist with assignments and prepare for tests
- Graded assignments, papers, and tests

Activities

February 2007–present

American College of Healthcare Executives, *Member*

August 2005–May 2007

The Pennsylvania State University, University Park, PA

- Member of the Master of Health Administration Association

Spring 2003–May 2005

Towson University, Towson, MD

- Member of the Towson University Healthcare Management Advisory Board

Index

A

Ability requirements, 9, 21, 74–75, 198–199
Accreditation, 36
Accreditation Association for Ambulatory Health Care (AAAHC), 36
ACHCA. *See* American College of Health Care Administrators
ACHE. *See* American College of Healthcare Executives
Aetna, 63
AHA. *See* American Hospital Association
AHIP. *See* America's Health Insurance Plans
ALFA. *See* Assisted Living Federation of America
ALFs. *See* Assisted living facilities
AMA. *See* American Medical Association
Ambulatory care organizations/clinics, 34–36, 202
American College of Health Care Administrators (ACHCA), 11
American College of Healthcare Executives (ACHE), 10, 11, 44, 47, 65
American College of Medical Practice Executives (ACMPE), 47
American Hospital Association (AHA), 40, 57
American Medical Association (AMA), 45, 57
American Public Health Association (APHA), 57
American Urological Association, 58
America's Health Insurance Plans (AHIP), 63
Analytical skills, 204
APHA. *See* American Public Health Association

Applied queuing theory, 35
ASAE and the Center for Association Leadership, 57, 59
Assisted living facilities (ALFs), 48–50, 201
Assisted Living Federation of America (ALFA), 48–49
Association of Children's Hospitals, 58
Association of State and Territorial Health Officers (ASTHO), 37–38
Association of University Programs in Health Administration (AUPHA), 7–8, 57–58
Associations, 57–59
ASTHO. *See* Association of State and Territorial Health Officers
AUPHA. *See* Association of University Programs in Health Administration

B

Bachelor of Science Healthcare Management (BS, HCMN), 3, 8
  advising form, 215–216
  sample program of study, 211–214, 217
Barr, K. W., 34
BearingPoint, 60
Beck, Larry M., profile of, 78–80
BLS. *See* Bureau of Labor Statistics
Boblitz, Michael C., profile of, 81–83
Bon Secours Health System, 43
Booz Allen Hamilton, 60
Breindel, C. L., 34
Brookdale Senior Living, 49
Buchbinder, S. B., 11
Bureau of Labor Statistics (BLS), 2, 3, 36, 58, 59, 65

C

CAE (Certified Association Executive), 59
Cardinal Health, 62
Catholic Healthcare West, 43
Cave, Sandy, profile of, 84–86
CCRCs. *See* continuing care retirement
    communities
Census Bureau, U.S., 10
Centers for Disease Control and Prevention
    (CDC), 37
Centers for Medicare and Medicaid Services
    (CMS), 27
Certification, 11
Certified Association Executive (CAE), 59
Certified Medical Practice Executive
    (CMPE), 47
Certified Nurse Aides/Nursing Assistants
    (CNAs), 52
Chisolm, Stephanie, profile of, 87–89
CIGNA Healthcare, 63
Clinics, 34–36, 202
CMPE. *See* Certified Medical Practice
    Executive
CMS. *See* Centers for Medicare and
    Medicaid Services
CNAs. *See* Certified Nurse Aides/Nursing
    Assistants
Command and control, 22
Commission on Accreditation of
    Healthcare Management Education
    (CAHME), 8
Communication skills, 21, 203, 205
Community hospitals, 40
Competencies of healthcare management,
    9, 21, 74–75, 198–199, 202–204
Conceptual skills, 21
Consulting firms, 59–61, 201
Continuing care retirement communities
    (CCRCs), 53–55, 201
Controlling function, 20
Council on Medical Education, 57
Council on Medical Services, 45
County health departments, 36–40
Cover letters, samples, 235–236, 239–240
Customer service skills, 35, 202

D

Data management, 201
Davis, Michael M., 3
Decision making, 21
Direct care settings, 33–56
    assisted living facilities, 48–50
    Beck, Larry M., profile of, 78–80
    Boblitz, Michael C., profile of, 81–83
    Cave, Sandy, profile of, 84–86
    definition of, 33–34
    Edwards, Teresa L., profile of, 93–95
    Forbes, William J., profile of, 102–103
    Fury, Schuyler, profile of, 108–111
    health departments, 36–40
    Honchar, Theresa C., profile of,
        112–113
    hospitals, 40–42
    hospital systems, 42–44
    Jones, Andrew, profile of, 114–116
    Jones, J. S. Parker, IV, profile of,
        117–119
    Kelley, Sharon E., profile of, 122–124
    Koontz, Lauren, profile of, 127–128
    Krauss, Jim, profile of, 129–130
    Llewellyn, Amanda, profile of,
        131–134
    Lyon, Lew, profile of, 137–139
    Maust, Karen, profile of, 144–146
    McDonnell, Michael J., profile of,
        147–149
    Neiswanger, Matt, profile of, 150–152
    nursing homes, 50–53
    Patel, Reena, profile of, 160–161
    physician practices, 44–48
    retirement communities, 53–55
    Richardson, Jeff, profile of, 165–166
    Street, Wes, profile of, 176–177
    Villani, Jennifer, profile of, 184–186
    wellness/fitness centers, 55–56
Directing function, 20
Diversity, 10
Doctoral degree programs, 3
Donovan, Kristi, profile of, 90–92
Drug companies, 65–66
Duncan, W. J., 27

E

Educational background, 3, 8–9, 198–199, 206. *See also* Bachelor of Science Healthcare Management (BS, HCMN); Master of Health Administration (MHA)

Edwards, Teresa L., profile of, 93–95

Elder care, 201

Emergency preparedness and response, 201

Emerging Leaders Program, 39, 40

Emeritus Senior Living, 49

Ernst and Young, 60

Ethics, 10–11

Experiential learning required, 12–13, 203, 204–205

External domains, 18, 19*t*

F

FACHE. *See* Fellowship of American College of Healthcare Executives

Fanning, Christopher, profile of, 96–97

Fearns, Valerie, profile of, 98–101

Federal agencies, job applications at, 38

Federal health departments, 36–40

Fellowship of American College of Healthcare Executives (FACHE), 11, 47

Fellowship of American College of Medical Practice Executives, 47

Field experience, 203

Finance skills, 204

Fitness centers, 55–56

Flexner, Abraham, 57

Forbes, William J., profile of, 102–103

Formal leadership development programs, 29

Fuller, Treg, profile of, 106–107

Functional organizational structure, 22, 23*f*

Functions of healthcare management, 20–21

Fury, Schuyler, profile of, 108–111

G

General education, 8–9

General Electric (GE), 62

Geriatrics, 201

Ginter, P. M., 27

Goals and objectives, 26–27, 203

Griffith, J. R., 27

Group medical practices, 45–46

H

HCA. *See* Hospital Corporation of America

HCR ManorCare, 49

Health and Human Services Department (HHS), 37, 38

Healthcare management (HCMN) programs, 7–9. *See also* Bachelor of Science Healthcare Management

Healthcare managerial positions, 41–42, 43–44

Health Care Services Corporation, 63

Health departments, 36–40

Health insurers, 63–65

HHS. *See* Health and Human Services Department

Honchar, Theresa C., profile of, 112–113

Hospital Corporation of America (HCA), 43

Hospitals and hospital systems, 40–44

Humana, 63

Human resources management, 26

I

Information technology, 201

Innovation skills, 204

Internal domains, 18, 19*t*

Internships, 13, 38, 203

Interpersonal skills, 21, 203, 205

Interviewing for jobs, 229–233

J

JCAHO. *See now* Joint Commission

Jobs in healthcare management, 221–242
    checklist for finding, 223–235
    FAQs, 221–224
    in federal agencies, 38
    interviewing, 229–233
    sample cover letters and résumés, 235–242
    terminology of advertisements and announcements, 224–229

Joint Commission (formerly JCAHO), 27, 36
Jones, Andrew, profile of, 114–116
Jones, J. S. Parker, IV, profile of, 117–119
Jurgensen, Michael, profile of, 120–121

K

Kaiser Family Foundation, 66
Kaiser Permanente, 63
Kelley, Sharon E., profile of, 122–124
Kellogg Foundation, 58
Kiser, Mary Beth, profile of, 125–126
Knowledge requirements, 7–9, 21, 74–75, 198–199
Kolb, D. A., 12
Koontz, Lauren, profile of, 127–128
Krauss, Jim, profile of, 129–130

L

Leadership development programs, 29
Liberal arts education, 8–9
Lifelong learning, 11, 47
Line managerial positions, 22
Llewellyn, Amanda, profile of, 131–134
Local health departments, 36–40
Loden, M., 10
Loeb, Jerod, profile of, 135–136
Long-term care, 201
Lyon, Lew, profile of, 137–139

M

Managed care organizations (MCOs), 45, 63–65, 202
Management
  career in, 3–13, 5–7t
  competencies, 9–11, 21, 35–36
  defined, 19
  functions, 20–21, 73–74
  key managerial skills required, 35–36, 46–47, 49
  need for management, 18–19
  organizational hierarchy, 21–24
  organization management, 24–25
  self-management, 24–25, 205
  succession planning, 28–29
  talent management, 26
  team management, 24–25
  types of positions, 19, 20t

unit management, 24–25
Manzanero, Natassja, profile of, 140–143
Maryland Conference of Local Environmental Health Directors, 38
Master of Health Administration (MHA), 8
  sample program of study, 219–220
Master of Public Health (MPH), 39
Master's degree programs, 3
Matrix models, 22, 24
Maust, Karen, profile of, 144–146
McDonnell, Michael J., profile of, 147–149
MCOs. See Managed care organizations
Medical College Admission Test (MCAT), 44
Medical Group Management Association (MGMA), 11, 47
Medical suppliers, 61–63
Medicare/Medicaid reimbursements, 52–53, 201
Medtronics, 62
Mentoring programs, 28–29, 197–198, 205
MGMA. See Medical Group Management Association
MHA. See Master of Health Administration
MPH. See Master of Public Health

N

National Committee for Quality Assurance (NCQA), 27
National Institutes of Health, 37
Neiswanger, Matt, profile of, 150–152
NHAs. See Nursing home administrators
Non-direct care settings, 57–66, 104–195
  associations, 57–59
  Chisolm, Stephanie, profile of, 87–89
  consulting firms, 59–61, 201
  defined, 33–34
  Donovan, Kristi, profile of, 90–92
  Fanning, Christopher, profile of, 96–97
  Fearns, Valerie, profile of, 98–101
  Fox, Harry, profile of, 104–195
  Fuller, Treg, profile of, 106–107
  Jurgensen, Michael, profile of, 120–121
  Kiser, Mary Beth, profile of, 125–126
  Loeb, Jerod, profile of, 135–136
  managed care organizations/health insurers, 45, 63–65, 202
  Manzanero, Natassja, profile of, 140–143

medical suppliers, 61–63
Novak, Ryan, profile of, 153–155
Papa, Ryan, profile of, 156–159
pharmaceutical firms, 65–66
Powell, Justine, profile of, 162–164
Saevoon, Andrea, profile of, 167–168
Shapiro, Jennifer R., profile of, 169–170
Sinha, Sunil K., profile of, 171–173
Skinner, Justin E., profile of, 174–175
Stull, Richard J., profile of, 178–180
Tyler, Jeanine, profile of, 181–183
Vollmer, Jason, profile of, 187–190
Woodard, Tanisha, profile of, 191–192
Novak, Ryan, profile of, 153–155
Nursing home administrators (NHAs), 51
Nursing homes, 50–53

O
Oral communication skills, 203
Organizational hierarchy, 21–24
Organizational level management, 24–25
Organizing function, 20

P
Papa, Ryan, profile of, 156–159
Patel, Reena, profile of, 160–161
Patient safety, 201
PCPs. *See* primary care physicians
Performance management, 26–28, 201
Performance measures, 27
Pharmaceutical firms, 65–66
PhRMA, 65
Physician practices, 44–48
Planning function, 20
Powell, Justine, profile of, 162–164
Practice settings, 33–70
    direct care settings, 33–56
    non-direct care settings, 33–34, 57–66
Primary care physicians (PCPs), 45, 202
Professional behavior, 10–11
Profiles of healthcare managers, 71–193.
    See also Direct care settings; Non-
    direct care settings
    ability requirements, 74–75, 198–199
    knowledge requirements, 74–75,
    198–199
    management functions, time spent on,
    73–74

sampling matrix and process for
    developing, 72
    satisfaction, sources of, 75–77, 196–197
    skills needed, 74–75, 198–199, 202–204
    typical day of, 73–77
Project management skills, 204
Public health, 36–40

Q
Quality improvement, 26–28, 201
Quiz on healthcare management talent
    quotient, 5–7t

R
Regulatory environment, 199
Rehabilitation facilities, 201
Reimbursement management, 199, 202
    Medicare/Medicaid reimbursements,
    52–53, 201
Relationship skills, 203, 205
Resources, 207–209
Résumés, samples, 237–238, 241–242
Retirement communities, 53–55
Richardson, Jeff, profile of, 165–166
Rosener, J. B., 10

S
Saevoon, Andrea, profile of, 167–168
Salaries. *See specific employment settings*
Satisfaction, sources of, 75–77, 196–197
Schön, D. A., 12
Self-management, 24–25, 205
Service line management models, 22, 24
Shapiro, Jennifer R., profile of, 169–170
Siemens, 62
Sinha, Sunil K., profile of, 171–173
Sisters of Mercy, 43
Skilled nursing facilities (SNFs), 51
Skills requirements, 9, 21, 74–75, 198–199
Skinner, Justin E., profile of, 174–175
Socioeconomic Monitoring System, 45
Staffing function, 20, 199–200
Staff managerial positions, 22
State health departments, 36–40
Street, Wes, profile of, 176–177
Stull, Richard J., 178–180, 206
Succession planning, 28–29
Sunwest Management, 49

Swayne, L. E., 27
Synthes, 62

T
Talent management, 26
Team-based models, 22, 24
Team level management, 11, 24–25
Technical skills, 21
Tenet Healthcare Corporation, 43
Thompson, J. M., 11
Turnover, 52
Tyler, Jeanine, profile of, 181–183
Typical day of healthcare managers, 73–77

U
United Health Group, 63
Unit level management, 24–25
University of Chicago, 3

V
Villani, Jennifer, profile of, 184–186
Vollmer, Jason, profile of, 187–190
Volunteerism, 203

W
Wellness/fitness centers, 55–56
Wellpoint, 63
W.K. Kellogg Foundation, 58
Woodard, Tanisha, profile of, 191–192
Work ethic, 203
Written communication skills, 203

X
Xavier University, 13

CPSIA information can be obtained
at www.ICGtesting.com
Printed in the USA
FFOW03n2332261215
19813FF

9 780763 759643